HOW TO ADD VALUE
TO YOUR HOME

HOW TO ADD VALUE
TO YOUR HOME

Scott McGillivray

Collins

How to Add Value to Your Home
Copyright © 2014 by Scott McGillivray.
All rights reserved.

Published by Collins,
an imprint of HarperCollins Publishers Ltd

First edition

Photographs appear courtesy of the author with the exception of the following: pages
74 and 93 courtesy iStockPhoto.com; page 106 courtesy Kidde Canada.

HarperCollins books may be purchased for educational, business
or sales promotional use through our Special Markets Department.

HarperCollins Publishers Ltd
2 Bloor Street East, 20th Floor
Toronto, Ontario, Canada
M4W 1A8

www.harpercollins.ca

Library and Archives Canada Cataloguing
Publication information is available upon request

ISBN 978-1-44341-058-8

Front cover photograph © Tim Leyes

Printed and bound in Canada
WEB 9 8 7 6 5 4 3

CONTENTS

INTRODUCTION

I am often asked how I got into real estate investing. The truth is, although my first purchase was a struggle, I was highly motivated to make it happen because I couldn't find any good rentals and I needed a place to live! The only way I could afford my first home was by having three roommates rent the other rooms in the house. My brother always told me, "necessity is the mother of all invention," and while that may be true, it was the discovery of rental income that was the "founding father" of my business.

As a proud homeowner and passionate property investor, I have learned a lot about real estate and, more importantly, its value. I teach about cash flow, income properties, and other investment techniques, but what produces some of the highest financial returns and has expedited the speed at which I have been able to grow wealth is most definitely the work I've put into increasing the value of my properties.

The value of real estate tends to increase in two ways. The first is market appreciation. Things like inflation, a growing economy, population growth and trends towards suburban or urban living can drive up the sticker price of homes. Market appreciation occurs over time and can work in reverse. The market crash of 2008, for example, caused *depreciation* in many U.S. housing markets. The important thing to remember about market appreciation is that you, as an individual homeowner, don't have any control over it.

The second way that real estate appreciates, however, is well within your control. "Forced appreciation" is the value that you add to your property through improvements, which include quality upgrades, updates and maintenance. The great thing about forced appreciation is that you can build on your investment as the market appreciates, but you can also protect your home's value when the housing market is in decline. Forced appreciation is how flippers and contractors who buy, renovate and sell properties as a business make their money. While fixing up a dilapidated house may be a good way to make a quick buck, why should the instant-gratification seekers make all the money? Homeowners can make even more money than the flippers, while at the same time enjoying their homes by making the right improvements.

It seems clear that many Canadians have recognized the role of smart renovations in the growing of home equity. In a recent Harris/Decima study, 39 percent of households reported plans to renovate some portion of their homes in the coming 12 months, and 74 percent of those said they were doing so, at least in part, in order to prepare their house for sale. They also planned to spend significant funds on these improvements—an average of just over $15,000.

Canadian financial institutions also feel strongly about the importance of real estate as a way to build personal wealth; so much so, in fact, that they have designed a number of financial tools to help people capitalize on their real estate investments. For example, most banks now offer mortgages that can be increased by the value of your home improvement renovations. In other words, banks are willing to finance renovations because they are confident in the returns that can be made by investing in real estate.

But whether you are borrowing money for home improvements or using your savings, you want to make sure that the money is being put to good use, not wasted. Ideally, you'd like to see that money build wealth in your home. But how do you do that?

Even if people aren't in a hurry to cash in on their homes, they may be embarking on renovations without really thinking about the long haul. And the long haul is where quality becomes so important. Some people feel that newer is better, no matter what. But there's an old saying that I like: *Only rich people can afford cheap things.* In other words, buying inexpensive, poorly made articles means that you will have to replace them often— something only people with a lot of cash are in the position to do. Renovations are much the same. There's a cheap version of everything out there, but if you opt for the inexpensive but inferior approach to projects, you may not save as much as you would think—you are likely to pay more for the labour (it's usually more difficult to work with flimsy or poorly made materials) as well as to incur the costs of repair work down the line. What's more, you can actually erase the value of your home's equity by taking shortcuts, by constructing things improperly or by doing the wrong renovations altogether. If you really want to gain the most from your investment in your home (and why wouldn't you?), then you want to make changes that will survive the test of time and be worth something in the future.

The *quality* of your renovations, however, is not the only key to maximizing your home's value and to profiting from the money you've spent on your property. Throughout this book, I make occasional references to renovation return-on-investment numbers that you may hear from appraisers, remodelling experts and the media. With the exception of painting, most of these numbers fall well below 100 percent. For example, you may hear that kitchens can get you 75 percent, but a new roof only 50 percent, meaning that, when you resell, you are going to earn back only a portion of the money you spent on the upgrades. Interestingly, while the Appraisal Institute of Canada used to publish these kinds of stats, it has abandoned the practice. Why? Because the numbers are unreliable, and there are just too many variables involved in home improvements to make these predictions very useful. I know this to be true. From my experience renovating and upgrading the properties I've owned, I have seen that you can earn back all of your investment—and even turn a profit on your upgrades—if you undertake home improvement in the right way. The "right way" involves three principles. As mentioned, quality counts. That's the first rule. But the consistency of your space is another essential factor in the equation. If you put a flashy, high-end bathroom into an otherwise dated and neglected home, you can't expect to fully recoup the reno costs or make a profit on the new work. If, however, that bathroom is complemented by updated, modern finishes and upgrades throughout the house, the whole package is going to increase in value in the eyes of prospective buyers. With home improvements, in other words, the whole is worth more than the sum of the parts.

The third key to maximizing the return you make on home reno investments is to make sure that your home improvements are in line with the market value of your property. That raises the question: How do you find out the market value of your home? Generally, you don't have to have an exact number in order to make decisions about renovations. The easiest way to get an idea, therefore, is to check the real estate listings in your neighbourhood and see what comparable houses are selling for. You may be tempted to use the assessment that your municipal government sends to you with your property tax bill. But this assessment is likely to be on the low side. Their calculation typically leaves out any renos that have been done without permits (like windows or flooring, updated bathrooms, etc.), general maintenance, finishes, landscaping and other aesthetics. The municipal assessment rarely reflects real market values.

If you want a more accurate sense of your home's worth, you can hire a professional licensed real estate appraiser. Professional appraisers will look at comparable properties in

This kitchen was in good shape but was tired and dated. We added new cupboard doors, hardware, a tiled backsplash, new appliances and a high-quality sink and faucet. We eliminated the bulkhead to create a more open space above the cupboards, which could then accommodate a valance and crown lighting. We also opted for an economical laminate countertop. We kept costs way down by using the existing floor plan, slate floor tiles and existing plumbing and heating. The cost of this luxurious-looking reno? Only $7,500!

your neighbourhood and then use a standard-deviation sheet to adjust for the differences between properties. Real estate agents will do much the same thing, but they tend to make these kinds of adjustments based on their instincts and previous experience. They can also factor in things that an appraiser might not include in his or her assessment—things like decor and landscaping, or the relative popularity of certain streets or locations, and so on.

Once you've got a sense of your home's potential price point, you can make informed decisions about how extensive or expensive your upgrades should be. If the housing prices in your neighbourhood are on the modest side, you may not find buyers who are willing to pay more for an expensive professional-grade cooktop and a walk-in wine cellar. On the flip side, if your home is in a high-end neighbourhood, a laminate kitchen countertop, no matter how new or stylish, might be a disappointment rather than an improvement in the eyes of buyers. Making home improvements that are appropriate to the value of your property and properties in your immediate area is essential to getting the greatest return on your home improvement investments.

Later in the book, I will talk about small things that you can do *immediately*, before you put your home on the market, to increase the likelihood that you will get the top price for your property. But these are small tweaks. Most of the things that you will do to increase the value of your home are bigger projects done over a number of years. Some of these things may be hard for prospective buyers to see and therefore appreciate. The best way to use this ongoing maintenance and improvement to sell your home is to "show" prospective buyers what you've done. You can do this by keeping detailed records of the work. This may include work permits, inspection reports, energy audits, service records, warranties, and renovation and repair contracts. I also highly recommend a photo record of any renovation or improvement, which means pictures of the work in progress as well as the finished project. When I was putting a deck on the back of my house, I photographed the footings as well as the support structure as I built, so I could show the quality of the work. I've also photographed things that will eventually be hidden behind drywall, like wiring, plumbing, beams, supports and insulation. It's a good idea to also document landscaping and to take photos of your garden at various points throughout the year so that homebuyers get idea of what the property looks like in all seasons. (Just make sure your yard looks its best before you snap the shutter.)

But I should make one thing really clear at the beginning of this book: home "improvements" and adding value to your home are not just a matter of renovations. More important, in fact, is maintenance. As the purchaser of hundreds of homes over the years, I look at the overall maintenance of a property before anything else. No matter how stylish or luxurious a space may appear, if it's not well maintained, all of the extras aren't worth it. The very foundation, then, of improving your home's value is consistent quality care of the basic structure and all its mechanics. So whenever you are thinking about home improvements, always factor maintenance costs into your overall budget. You don't want to add a gleaming new kitchen and then have no cash to fix a leaking roof.

And that leads us to the question of money. To maximize the value you add to your home, you have to consider not just what you can spend, but what you *should* spend. To do that, many experts suggest that you need to determine how long you are going to stay in your home. If you are planning to move in two to five years, you should look at the return on investment of every dollar you shell out on improvements—in other words, don't spend a lot of money that you can't recoup. After all, even a quality kitchen reno might get back only 75 percent of its cost. If you plan on staying in your home for eight years or longer, you can consider renovations that don't provide as much of a return, and some things that are "just for you." There is nothing wrong with splurging on extras that may not give you a financial uptick on resale but that you will enjoy while you are living in the home—as long as you realize that this is the choice you are making.

Yes, if you want to increase the value of your home, you have to spend your money wisely. But that being said, I need to point out that this doesn't mean cutting corners or nickel-and-diming every decision that comes your way. When you are embarking on any reno, it can be a mistake to choose the least expensive options, thinking you may upgrade at a later date. Take it from me: that later date never comes, and you end up living with finishes or fixtures you've never been happy with, or you find yourself having to do more work and spending more money than you want to so as to get your house ready to show.

And one more word of advice: before you embark on costly renos, consider the difference between adding value to your home and adding value to your net worth. As I've pointed out, certain renovations and maintenance are necessary to avoid devaluing your property, but what about renos that are meant to boost your house resale price?

On my show, *Income Property*, we always outline the costs of the renovations and have the homeowners weigh them against the income that will be generated by the resulting rental suite. At the end of the renovation, we also get a real estate agent in to give us an estimate of how much the house has increased in value. It seems pretty straightforward. Well, in truth, it is . . . and it isn't. What we really can't address fully on the show is the individual financial situation of every homeowner. Some may have money put aside for the improvements. Some may be borrowing from family to cover the renovations. Others may be getting a bank loan. While we can't divulge our participants' personal finances, you can be sure that *they* factor those variables into their calculations when they decide what level of renovation they want to start.

Even if you aren't calculating the cost and benefit of a new income suite in your home, any sort of renovation or improvement needs some involved number crunching. Putting in a bright new $30,000 kitchen may raise your property value by $30,000, but if you are borrowing that money (perhaps taking out an equity loan on the house), you haven't really gained anything if you aren't able to pay off the loan in a timely fashion. You should always factor in the cost of borrowing any money you need. When it comes to home renovations, there are several different ways of financing them, and although a great scenario is that you have the money available in savings, that's not the only way to make improvements to your home. If you are going to finance your renovation, there are some great products available that are most appropriate for home renovations, and because your home is an asset, most institutions have a series of options available to you. You may want to look at financing the renovations through a secured line of credit or even roll it into your mortgage to ensure you get the lowest interest rate on the funds. The key here is affordable financing. Think of it this way: many people think nothing of running up their high-interest credit card for renovation materials, whereas a home renovation line of credit has an interest rate that is a fraction of that. Because you'll be doing improvements that will increase value, it should be money well spent and may even make you money if you make the right choices. Remember that the total of what you are going to spend has to include the interest you will pay over the life of the loan. And if you are considering an income suite, the interest on any renovation money you borrow has to be put against the rent you will be collecting. (I usually suggest that, if you borrow money to put in an income suite, you be able to pay off this loan within two years to five years to make the investment worthwhile.)

You will also need to add in any additional maintenance costs that your changes might incur. For example, there is obviously considerable cost involved in the upkeep of a new pool, but an addition will also cost extra money to heat and maintain. By contrast, new windows might be pricey, but you can factor in the energy savings you'll get from the added insulation. Whatever changes you execute, you should be making sure you are thinking about the *real* price. You might also want to look at the "opportunity cost" of your changes. For example, think about the number of years of enjoyment you will get from that feature. Then you can divide the total cost by the years to see how much that hot tub, built-in wine cooler or skylight will cost you per year. Is it worth it to you?

Finally, you may notice in the following pages that I often caution against spending a lot of money on renos that are unusual, quirky or just highly individual. And you might ask what I've got against originality or personal choice. Well, nothing, to be honest. But in this book, my focus is on how to increase the value of your home, so my advice is always given with a mind towards what the market—in other words, homebuyers—are looking for. And the fact is, the more people who are interested in your property, and who like the features your home has to offer, the higher the price you will be able to command for your home when you want to sell it. Think of it this way: a year ago, you spent $30,000 putting in a beautiful new pool in your backyard, while your next-door neighbour spent the same on a state-of-the-art kitchen. Now you have both put your homes on the market. Your homes are the same size, on comparable lots, with more or less the same features, with the exception of the new pool and the new kitchen. Fifty people come through the properties. Almost everyone loves the new kitchen, but only two people are looking for a house with a pool. And worse, at least a dozen of the people won't even consider a home with a pool because they don't want the work and expense of keeping it up. Your neighbour ends up with multiple offers and a bidding war for the house. You get one offer—which doesn't give you a lot of room to negotiate. No doubt about it, your neighbours will end up with more money in their pockets at the end of the day. And while the pool/kitchen example is a little obvious, the same principle holds true for all sorts of other home upgrades. So if you are concerned about getting as much money back as possible on the renovations when you sell your home, or you want to make sure that changes always increase your home's value, you are going to want to make improvements that you like *and* that others will too—whether it's paint colours or bathroom fixtures. That way, you will improve both your home and your net worth.

Chapter 1

DIY OR CONTRACTOR?

It can be a little tricky talking about projects that could be good "do-it-yourself" jobs because all DIY depends on a person's comfort with tools, skill level and attention to detail. I know people who are capable of doing pretty major renovations in their spare time, but I've also seen the simplest home improvements, like installing a towel bar or painting a wall, botched by someone who simply isn't handy. Before embarking on any do-it-yourself home improvements, you need to make an honest inventory of your resources, your skills and your aptitude for this kind of work.

Most DIY projects require you to have a few tools. For the simplest tasks, this may entail the right size of screwdriver or a good paintbrush and tray. More involved projects might require more specialized tools or power tools. But tools are not usually a make-or-break factor in a DIY project. If you don't have the necessary equipment, you can usually borrow or rent it. What *is* important is your capability, as well as your willingness to take the time to do a job properly and safely. If you are the type of person who will research how to do something, follow instructions carefully and make sure that the work is done thoroughly and meticulously, then DIY may work for you. Remember that with really big projects, you will also need a significant amount of time, and you may need more than one pair of hands. If you are able to work only in the evenings and on weekends, the job is going to take you more time than it would with a full-time crew. Can you and your family tolerate the ongoing inconvenience and mess?

Of course, if you do any of your home-improvement labour yourself, you will likely save more money on the upgrade and thus make more money on resale. This is particularly true of small jobs, as contractors will always charge a minimum amount for any project they take on.

So how do you decide which projects need a professional and which can be DIY projects? As long as you get the necessary building permits and inspections, you can legally do just about any sort of renovation on your house. But interestingly, in most municipalities, you are not legally permitted to do many of the same things to someone else's home. This can be a good way to determine what kinds of jobs should be done by a professional in your home as well. Municipal licensing for renovators is usually required for:

- waterproofing a foundation;
- bricklaying;
- roofing;
- siding;
- drywalling.

As mentioned above, you can do these kinds of jobs in your own home, but it is probably worth the money to get a licensed professional to do the work so that your home improvements are quality ones that will both look good and stand the test of time.

Other renovations and home upgrades require a licensed tradesperson to complete the work. These are jobs that I do *not* recommend you undertake yourself. They include:

- electrical work;
- plumbing;
- HVAC (heating, ventilation and air conditioning);
- structural changes (removing or adding walls, building additions, etc.).

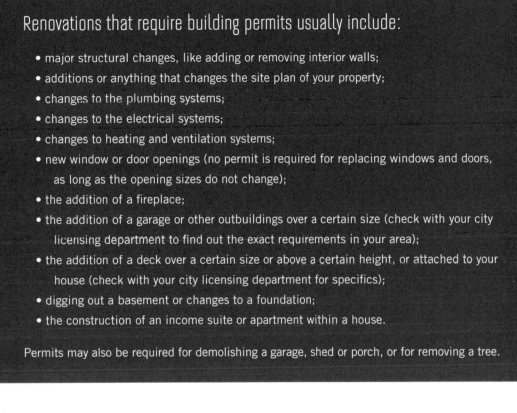

Renovations that require building permits usually include:

- major structural changes, like adding or removing interior walls;
- additions or anything that changes the site plan of your property;
- changes to the plumbing systems;
- changes to the electrical systems;
- changes to heating and ventilation systems;
- new window or door openings (no permit is required for replacing windows and doors, as long as the opening sizes do not change);
- the addition of a fireplace;
- the addition of a garage or other outbuildings over a certain size (check with your city licensing department to find out the exact requirements in your area);
- the addition of a deck over a certain size or above a certain height, or attached to your house (check with your city licensing department for specifics);
- digging out a basement or changes to a foundation;
- the construction of an income suite or apartment within a house.

Permits may also be required for demolishing a garage, shed or porch, or for removing a tree.

Choosing a Contractor

So, you know you need some professional help, but how do you know whom to hire? The best way to find contractors or design-build firms is through referrals. Ask friends and neighbours if they have worked with anyone they can recommend. There are a number of advantages in approaching contractors who have worked with your neighbours. You can easily take a look at the finished projects they have done in your neighbours' homes. And the contractors will know the neighbourhood and will have worked with the local inspectors. You should contact or investigate, one way or another, at least 10 different contractors. That may sound like a lot, but even if you contact all 10, you are likely to get only half that number to the house to give you an estimate. (Some may be too busy, some may not be interested in the scope of the work, and others may not show up for some other reason.)

And out of the five who show up, you'll be lucky to get estimates from three of them. Others might find the job too big or too small, or may not like the budget you are working with. Keep in mind that the quotes you are gathering from the contractors will not cover the scope of the work in detail at this time; rather, they will be very basic estimates that will usually give a dollar range with a very general description of the work based on what you have told them you want (such as "kitchen renovation with new cabinets, tile backsplash and flooring, existing walls, plumbing and windows").

When choosing a contractor, many people focus on those estimates. You may have heard the advice that you should toss out the highest and lowest and go with one of the middle quotations. But price shouldn't be your first consideration. (Remember, these are only ballpark numbers. A lot can change by the time you've completed a total scope of work and the renovation itself.)

The most important thing to consider when choosing a contractor is character. When the contractors come to inspect your home and look at the project, take the opportunity to interview them. Did you like them? Did you feel comfortable with them? Did you feel as if you were all communicating well—that they understood what you were asking for and you understood what they had to say? A home renovation can be a long project with dozens, if not hundreds, of decisions to be made along the way. It's essential that you like and trust the professionals you are hiring and that you feel comfortable having them in your home day after day.

The second thing to consider is how thorough the estimate is. As mentioned earlier, it will not cover a complete scope of the work, but you want the quotation to reflect the upgrades you are looking for. An extremely vague quotation may indicate that the contractor is not serious about undertaking the job, hasn't been paying attention to what you want or isn't factoring in things he or she knows will need to be done, even if you don't. (For example, doing a full kitchen reno in an older home may involve replacing interior plumbing or significantly upgrading the electrical work. A good contractor will advise you about these kinds of considerations while discussing your plans.)

The third thing to think about when making your decision is the cost. Chances are the estimates you have gathered will vary wildly. I don't usually consider the lowest estimate; any quote that is considerably less than the others I receive is likely *not* to have included all of the things I have asked for or that are needed.

It's a good idea to ask for references as well as photos of the contractor's previous work—especially jobs that are similar in scope to yours. Also make sure that your contractor has a proper operating licence and that the tradespeople he or she will be employing have the appropriate licences. Your contractor—and any subcontractors he or she will be using—should also carry workers' compensation and liability insurance.

Once you have chosen the contractor you would like to work with, it's time to ask him or her for a detailed scope of work. The estimate is no longer the document you will be working with. The scope of work should include:

- all of the work that will be completed, as well as all work that will *not* be done or will be done by the owners (for example, demolition and cleanup—will you be doing this or the contractor?);
- all materials that will be used and a price range for them (with a note that owners will pay if materials are in excess of this amount or will receive a credit if the materials cost less);
- a list of permits needed and who will be responsible for obtaining the permits;
- a detailed schedule for the work, with precise start and finish dates and agreements about what will happen if timelines are not met;
- a breakdown of the costs for each phase or major aspect of the job;
- a payment schedule.

To see examples of an estimate and scope of work, visit www.scottmcgillivray.com.

The payment schedule should include a number of instalments, usually payable at the commencement of work, when rough-in inspections are passed, and when final inspections are passed. A deposit is sometimes requested, but this should be no more than 10 percent of the total. It's also a good idea to make the final instalment due only after both parties have done a final walk-through of the finished project. You should never pay up front for an entire renovation job, no matter how modest.

The scope of work is the basis of your renovation agreement with the contractor, but you should not think of it as the final and complete contract. The nature of renovating means that unexpected problems and issues are to be *expected*. I don't know if I've ever worked on a renovation where there hasn't been some little surprise along the way. Sometimes it's a problem, like slowly leaking pipes, that only reveals itself once the walls are down or the floor opened up. Sometimes it's a previous upgrade or repair that wasn't done properly. And other times, it's finding work that might have been acceptable at the time the house was built but now is simply not up to code. On top of those sorts of additional jobs, you may well find things that you want to do that hadn't occurred to you when the original scope of the renovation was discussed. All of these changes should be documented with "change of work orders" that are drawn up, with the new work described and a fee invoiced, and added to the original scope of work. These combined documents now serve as the working contract. I have to admit, if you aren't prepared for them, these change of work orders can be a bit of a shock. I've done projects where the costs invoiced on the change orders added up to more than the original scope of work cost! That's why many people recommend that you budget 25 percent more than the original quoted cost of the renovation when you embark on a major home upgrade.

And finally, do you need to hire an architect, designer or structural engineer for a major home renovation? Of course, the more people you hire, the more expensive the job will be. But major renovations that require building permits also need the involvement of these professionals. The easiest way to go is to hire a design-build firm that either has architects or engineers on staff or can subcontract and include these services as part of the work so you don't have to assemble and manage the team yourself. The architects will draw up the plans, including things like building specs, fire doors, insulation, vapour barrier, lighting and electrical outlets, wall assemblies and so on. The designers will take measurements, help pick colours and finishes, and may even be able to render the floor plans. Engineers are required to plan and approve the structural elements of the building—for example, spans and loads and related specifications. Once the plans are finalized, they must be approved by the city. When the plans are approved and building permits issued, the licensed general contractor will hire the tradespeople to execute all of these plans. The contractor will also organize all of the inspections that need to take place. Inspections of plumbing, ductwork and exposed structural changes will be conducted by city inspectors. Electrical inspections are done by the

Electrical Safety Authority (ESA). If the inspectors have specified that changes need to be made in order for the work to pass, the contractor will work with the engineer, architect and trades to make the changes, and a second round of inspections will be scheduled.

For more on planning renovations and working with contractors, check out my website: www.scottmcgillivray.com.

Chapter 2

KITCHENS

As a real estate investor and landlord, I look at hundreds of houses a year. And what is the first thing I notice? The kitchen. Every time I bring prospective tenants through one of my properties, they head straight to the kitchen too.

Today, the kitchen is the centre of the home—whether for food preparation, taking meals or just hanging out, it's where we spend a lot of our time. So it makes sense that helping the kitchen to shine goes a long way toward increasing the value of your home. It's an important place to invest your home improvement bucks. In its 2013 Cost vs. Value Report, the U.S. magazine *Remodeling* noted that a minor kitchen remodel will average a 75 percent return on investment, while a major one will recoup about 60 percent. But I know that it's possible to achieve closer to 200 percent if you know what you are doing and if the kitchen reno is part of a well-maintained and upgraded home. The kitchen is the most valuable room in a home, so if you want to increase the value of your home, this is the first place to focus your attention.

Before getting started, you have to evaluate how much work is needed to maximize your returns. A high ROI will only be realized if the renovation is appropriate to the house. Real estate, renovation and appraisal experts throw around various ratios of kitchen reno costs to the value of your home. I've heard some recommend that you spend no more than 3 percent of your current house value on kitchen updates (for example, $12,000 on a $400,000 property), and I've seen recommendations as high as 25 percent (or $100,000 on a $400,000 property) to get the best returns. I think those last numbers are crazy. A lavish $100,000 chef's kitchen in a $300,000 or $400,000 house just doesn't make sense—especially if you are hoping to get a return on investment of 100 percent or more. I like to stay within 5 to 10 percent, keeping in mind that there are variables with every situation. If you live in an area of the country with modest housing costs, and your current kitchen really needs a full reno and not a facelift, you may find it difficult to get a new kitchen layout, cabinets, countertops, flooring and appliances for 5 percent of your house's value. If, however, you live in an area where housing prices are high, 10 percent may be more than you need to spend to get a quality kitchen appropriate to your house. So before you start, spend a little time thinking about your budget, pricing out different options and calculating what your home is worth in the current resale market. That's the only way to ensure that you increase the value of your home as much as you can.

And part of those calculations involves deciding what type of kitchen improvement you want and need. I like to think in terms of three "levels": basic upgrade, refacing and replacing.

The Basic Upgrade

This first level of improvement is based on having an existing kitchen that essentially functions well but needs a facelift. That means you are leaving the layout and the cabinet structure as-is but freshening the finishes and perhaps replacing the appliances. Depending on what needs to be done, this level of improvement can cost several thousands of dollars—or less than $100.

Don't be fooled into thinking bigger or more elaborate is better when it comes to renovations. The basic kitchen upgrade (versus the more involved kitchen makeovers discussed below) can offer the best return on investment because you spend relatively little to create a substantially new look. With the basic upgrade, you may achieve returns of up to 200 percent if all goes well. That's a $4,000 increase in value with only $2,000 spent on improvements.

HARDWARE

What's the best bang for your buck in a kitchen? Change out the cabinet hardware!

The knobs and pulls on the cabinets are the first thing people notice or touch in the kitchen. Dated, flimsy or damaged hardware makes the whole kitchen feel that way. That's why, even if I am planning to put in a whole new kitchen in a year, I'll still replace the hardware as soon as I acquire the property.

A basic kitchen reno can still produce a high-end look. We added eight flat pack cabinets but kept the rest of the original floor plan. Spraying the old cabinets ourselves and adding the distinctive gold hardware gave us a very big bang for a very small buck. The most expensive part of the kitchen reno was the marble countertop, but we kept costs low by using the slab offcut to make the six-inch backsplash.

These days, most hardware stores have a good variety of modern, stylish knobs and pulls to choose from at reasonable prices. Just make sure that you stick with something simple and elegant if your concern is upping the value of your home—the knife-and-fork drawer pulls are fun, but they won't appeal to everyone. (Of course, you can always go for the knife-and-fork pulls, but replace them before you plan to sell the house.)

If you have only knobs on your kitchen cabinets, you can usually replace with either knobs or handles. Handles will require a second hole, but usually you can position them so that you can use the existing hole as well. If you are replacing handles with handles, bring the old pulls with you when shopping or measure the distance between the two holes so that you get the right size to fit the existing holes in your cabinets.

PAINT

Replacing the knobs and pulls with new ones is the simplest, most cost-effective DIY project you can take on. And next on the list of simple and frugal upgrades: painting. Choose an eggshell finish for the walls, but don't stop there. Also consider whether the cabinetry could be spruced up with a coat of cabinet paint. This is another great do-it-yourself project.

COUNTERTOPS

Because countertops are working surfaces, they can really show their age—and really date a place. But replacing them usually requires only a modest investment. Most countertops can be easily popped off, so depending on what kind of new surface you choose, this can be a quick DIY project.

Laminates come with the lowest price point in countertops and are available at almost any hardware or home-reno store. They also come in a huge range of colours, styles, patterns and textures. Laminates have evolved a lot in recent years, and there are some very high-quality products now available. Since even the most expensive laminates are so reasonably priced, I recommend investing more than a couple of hundred bucks on your laminate and going for a higher-end, good quality product. Choosing a premium laminate will still get you great value for your money.

I prefer to use laminate slab countertops (no attached backsplash). The slab design allows more flexibility when adding a backsplash to the wall. Laminates are either ordered to size, which is a straightforward installation, or need to be cut to fit. If you are cutting the countertop yourself, be sure to purchase the matching edge banding (strips of flexible laminate), which can be cut to cap any open cuts on the edges of the countertop (hiding the core). The edge banding is typically pre-glued and applied with a heat gun. Once the countertop is screwed in place; the sink cutout is the only other modification that is usually needed.

Composite Countertops

Engineered stone and composite countertops are pricier than laminates (they can range from mid-price to very expensive), but they are another excellent choice. Some, like Silestone, Caesarstone and Zodiaq, are made from stone dust (usually quartz) and a polymer resin; others, like Corian and Gibraltar, are composed of acrylic or polyester resins and fillers. Either variety comes in a wide range of colours and patterns. Engineered countertops are attractive, durable and consistent—you can look at samples and know exactly what you are going to get. It is easy to custom-size these products, and they can be made with built-in sinks. Another bonus is that they're usually seamless. Better still, engineered countertops need very little maintenance. Small nicks and burns can be buffed out, and countertops made from polyurethanes can be repaired with a heat gun. Plus, since the material is solid and the countertop is cut for the sink, you can usually ask that these leftover pieces be made into cutting boards for you (the manufacturers will usually do it for free).

Natural Stone

Granite countertops are increasingly popular. They lend your kitchen an air of luxury and sophistication. But they do come in a range of prices (from mid-price to super-high), and you probably want to avoid countertops at the bottom of the price scale. Granite countertops that have been cut too thin are likely to crack. And of course, being slabs of natural stone, every piece of granite will be a little different. If you are opting for granite, you really should go to the warehouse and pick the exact piece you want, keeping in mind where variations in the stone will appear once the slab is made into a countertop.

Marble is another natural stone that can be used for kitchen countertops. Bakers love the surface for rolling out pastry. But marble is a softer, more porous stone than granite, so it's prone to scratches, nicks and staining. That's why you'll see it used more often in bathrooms,

Kitchen DIY Projects

There are a number of kitchen upgrades that may be do-it-yourself jobs, depending on your skill and aptitude. You might be able to switch out the kitchen faucet. It's always simplest if you pick one that is the same format as your previous faucet, so if you have a widespread fixture, go with a new widespread set; a single-hole design replaces another single-hole faucet; and so on. If, however, you have a standard or widespread handle and faucet setup, and you want to convert to a single-hole style, there are escutcheon plates that can be used to cover the extra holes. If you do plan to change out a faucet set on your own, make sure you shut off the water to the kitchen sink. If there isn't a shut-off valve leading to the sink, you will have to shut off the main water valve to the house, but I also highly recommend adding a shut-off valve under the sink while you are replacing the faucet.

You may also be able to install a range hood and drill the hole for its ventilation yourself, or install a laminate countertop (see below).

Another job that you may want to do yourself is adding or replacing a kitchen backsplash. Later in the book, I will advise you *not* to attempt a large tiling job (like a shower stall or a floor) on your own. Tiling is trickier than it looks, and in large areas, mistakes in alignment and grouting are obvious. But small areas, like a backsplash, are more forgiving. Tiling for backsplashes is also available in sheets, which makes installation easier. (I would still say you need to score eight out of 10 on your DIY skill set to take this on.)

Installing kitchen cabinets can be a DIY project, but you need to have some general building experience and a firm understanding of how to find structure within your walls so that cabinets can be properly secured. This is especially important in older homes with lath and plaster walls where the lath may appear to be structural when screwed into. You also need to understand the details that comprise a quality kitchen upgrade—like a gable panel above and beside the fridge, 24-inch-deep cabinets above a fridge, and the absence of any gaps between cabinets or between cabinets and walls. Remember that any crooked cabinets, gaps or awkward layouts will be a red flag to prospective homebuyers. If the kitchen looks like it has undergone an unprofessional renovation, the quality of the rest of the house and its improvements will be called into question.

Kitchen upgrades that are *not* DIY jobs, in my opinion, are structural changes and electrical or plumbing upgrades.

Replacing Knobs and Cabinet Painting

Materials needed: knobs, screws, cabinet paint, painter's masking tape, wood filler, sandpaper, trisodium phosphate (TSP) cleaner, and maybe new hinges.
Tools needed: screwdriver, paintbrush and rollers, paint sprayer and compressor, cabinet repainting kit.

The best and easiest DIY jobs in the kitchen are replacing the cabinet knobs and handles, and painting the kitchen cabinets. All you need for the knobs is a handheld screwdriver and about 30 seconds.

For cabinet painting, choose a melamine paint or a paint with a melamine component to improve durability. To prep the cabinets before painting, remove the doors and give the boxes and the doors a little sanding. You may also want to fill knob and handle holes with a little wood filler and then sand this down once it has dried. After sanding, I like to scrub the boxes and doors with a TSP cleaner. (Also, when removing the knobs and hinges, tape the screws to the hardware they came from so that they don't get lost and so that everything is easy to put back when the painting is finished.) Most hardware stores sell a cabinet repainting kit with paint, sponges, brushes and instructions for a reasonable price. For a more professional look, you can also use a compressor with a sprayer to get a more even finish or opt to take the doors off and have them sprayed at a shop for only a few hundred dollars. This professional work will give you a more consistent finish with no drips or brush marks. When painting cabinetry, I spray a primer coat first and let it dry a few days before spraying the top paint. Cabinet paint can take up to 30 days to dry fully, so be careful around newly painted cabinetry. But however you choose to do it, you'll be amazed at how a few coats of paint will transform the space.

You can also quickly and cheaply update the look of your cabinets by adding or removing trim—for example, adding straight-square rails to flat cabinet fronts will give you a great shaker look.

where the countertops don't get quite the same workout as their kitchen counterparts. If you do opt for marble, seal it well and often (once every three to four months is often suggested), wipe up stains immediately—especially acidic foods, red wine, etc.—and never use it as a cutting surface. Another way to go is to confine it to a small area, such as an island, and use extra caution when prepping food there.

There are other natural stones to choose from as well, but many have significant problems with staining, chipping or durability. Some are quite difficult, and therefore expensive, to install. And I'm not a big fan of anything that is particularly porous, uneven or unusual. You may end up opting for a natural stone other than granite or marble, but this will probably be a "just for you" choice. In other words, don't expect to recoup the full value of what this countertop cost to purchase and install.

"Just for You/Personal Choice/The Extras" Countertop Choices
Concrete
Concrete countertops are usually made on site, with a mixture of concrete, additives and often dyes. They are reinforced with various materials and must be sealed after they have cured. The surface can also be ground or polished to give the material a sleek look. Concrete countertops are tough, heat-resistant and stain-resistant, and they have a striking, almost industrial look—which can be a good complement to a contemporary kitchen design.

I have never installed one—and I'll tell you why. First, these countertops are heavy, and you need to know that both the cabinets and the structure of your kitchen can support the weight. And they are time-consuming to install as well as tricky to pour and finish, so you need to have someone with extensive experience making these for you. But more than anything, the reason I have avoided these countertops is that they are uncommon and unusual—and when it comes to increasing the value of your home, those are not necessarily positive traits. A lot of people considering your property are going to be wondering about how they maintain and care for those countertops, not to mention who they will contact should the countertop need repair. And the look of a concrete countertop can be quite masculine or industrial, an aesthetic that doesn't allow for a lot of design or decorating versatility. Concrete countertops can be visually striking, but I really feel their appeal is limited.

Stainless Steel

The same holds true for stainless steel countertops. They can give a kitchen a sleek, commercial look. If your entire property fits this aesthetic (say, a converted industrial loft space), then these countertops, like concrete ones, might be an appropriate choice. But water, spills and crumbs show up very obviously on stainless steel countertops—as do the nicks and scratches they can be prone to. So despite the hygienic qualities of these countertops, I would limit stainless steel to the appliances in a family home.

Tiled Countertops

Even though tiled countertops are much more common than concrete or stainless steel, I'm not a fan of them, either. But worse, tiled countertops can crack and chip, and repairing them, even if you have plenty of leftover tiles, can be a real pain. And while ceramic tile is easy enough to clean, the grout between the tiles isn't, meaning it often gets stained and dirty-looking. If you really love the look of tiled countertops, keep the grout lines as thin as possible to avoid this problem. But really, I recommend keeping the tiles to the backsplash or the floor.

Butcher's Block and Sealed Wood

An unvarnished hardwood butcher block can be nice to work on—like one big cutting board. But this is not really an appropriate choice for a whole countertop, as the wood should not be near sink areas and is not particularly resistant to heat. What's more, it will score and mark fairly easily (especially if used as a cutting board), so it needs to be sanded regularly if you want to maintain a smooth surface. A butcher-block countertop works best in a contained area, like a small island, or as an accent in conjunction with other countertops. Most butcher-block countertops will require sealing. Use a mineral oil to protect them and apply annually to maintain its look.

Varnished or sealed hardwood countertops are not particularly common but may be a tempting choice if you have a country-style kitchen. But I think the cons outweigh the warm look they lend a space. Coated wood can scratch and nick quickly (so should not be used as a cutting board) and is not particularly heat-resistant. And it is no easier to clean than laminates or engineered surfaces. If you like the warmth of wood, opt for wood cabinets and choose something more versatile for your countertops.

Using more than one countertop material can break up a space, create depth and interest and give you more bang for your buck. Here we chose a laminate around the sink and stove and a wood butcher block for the island.

One final thought about countertops: the standard height for kitchen counters is 36 inches. Short or tall people may be tempted to play with that height. Custom cabinets can be built accordingly. Flat box cabinets can sometimes be raised with legs but can't really be cut down. But before you decide to veer from the standard measurements, consider how long you will be staying in your home. If you are thinking of selling in five to eight years, you would be best to stick with standard heights.

BACKSPLASHES

The backsplash is a kitchen detail that is completely optional. Kitchens can look great without them, and as long as the paint you've used on the walls behind your counter is a good-quality, washable one, you shouldn't have a problem keeping the area clean and fresh-looking. But backsplashes can be a relatively inexpensive way to add a little flair to your kitchen. There are hundreds of options for backsplashes—all sorts of tile, glass, pressed tin, stainless steel sheets and more—but I don't like to get too fancy with this area. As well, some of these options can be pricey and difficult to install. To get the most value out of your space, the countertop should be the star—the backsplash is just a supporting actor.

Basic ceramic tiles are very popular because the options are endless. But these days, I tend to use a lot of marble tile. It gives the counter area a clean, timeless look. And while you can go with very inexpensive tiles and still get a good look, since this is such a small area, upping the ante and getting what you want won't cost you a lot extra (I try to spend no more than $10 a square foot). In fact, fancier tiles for a backsplash are likely to cost you only a few hundred dollars extra versus the thousands extra it might cost you to go for a more expensive countertop option. (One word of caution: you have to be careful installing a marble tile backsplash. Since marble is veined and porous, it tends to crack when applied to uneven surfaces, like the walls in many older homes.)

But even simple or plain tile can be used to great effect on a backsplash. Rectangular tiles can be arranged in a herringbone or brick pattern. Plain tiles can be dressed up with a detailed accent tile placed in intervals along the backsplash. But resist the urge to do massive inlays (behind the stovetop, for example) or personalize the look too much. (More than once, I've walked into a kitchen to find a farm scene or some such thing in tiles over the stove. And my first thought was always about how much work it was going to be to get rid of it.) Remember, your backsplash shouldn't fight your countertop for attention but should complement it. You want to keep the look simple, elegant and classic to maximize your return on investment.

SINKS AND FAUCETS

If you are changing your countertops, then changing your sink is an easy upgrade. The double sink is the standard in most kitchens—and is usually the most appropriate choice. A large chef-style kitchen may feature two sinks—a large one and a small prep sink in a different location. Some people do opt for one big sink on its own (the apron front or farm sink can make for a nice look in some kitchens), but if you are going to go that route, just make sure you have a dishwasher. Otherwise, dishwashing can be more of a chore than it needs to be.

Sinks are made from a lot of different materials these days, but don't let a sink blow your kitchen budget. When considering return on investment, your best bet is going to be a quality stainless steel model. That modifier, "quality," is important. Stainless steel comes in a range of gauges. To make sure the sink is durable and stays good-looking, avoid the thinnest gauges and spend a little more for heavier steel. Surface-mount stainless sinks are the standard, but if you are installing granite, stone or composite countertops, do go for the undermount sink style for a clean, contemporary look.

Even if you don't replace your sink, you can replace your faucet as long as you purchase a unit that fits the holes that are already present in your sink and countertop. Kitchen faucets range from $50 to well over $1,000, but you really don't need to go to the high end of the price range. There are lots of good-quality, attractive choices for under $200.

APPLIANCES

Your kitchen appliances, whether you are thinking of selling or staying, should always be in good working order. And replacing dated or non-functioning appliances is an easy upgrade—but not always an inexpensive one. Just keep in mind when you are shopping for new appliances that you don't have to buy the most expensive or the cheapest machines on the market. What's really important is that the appliances you choose are appropriate for your space. Just as the kitchen should reflect the value of your property, so too should your appliances reflect the value of your kitchen and your house. A top-of-the-line industrial-quality range is overkill in a modest suburban house. If you do opt for this type of appliance, it has got to be for personal enjoyment and not property resale value. But if you are wavering about how much to spend, err on the side of quality.

When it comes to getting new appliances, you need to focus on the oven and the refrigerator. And for both of these, you should make sure that you are getting the right style, the right size and the right width for your kitchen. For example, refrigerators come in a variety of widths and heights; while they are most commonly about 30 inches wide, this dimension can range all over the map. You don't want to spend a fortune on a new fridge, only to have it stick out eight inches past the area you had set aside for it, or have a huge gap on either side of it. Take all of your kitchen measurements when you go shopping. You also want to make sure that the door swings in the right direction—or that it comes with a switch kit so you can change the swing if need be.

Appliances are not just functional—they also serve as an aesthetic element in your home. They are, in a sense, furniture for your kitchen. That's why, in every kitchen I do, I make sure that appliances match—in colour, style and, if possible, brand. If you are trying to sell your home, most people who look at it are going to be thinking that they have to replace the appliance that doesn't look the same as the rest. Matching appliances eliminate that concern and give your whole kitchen a put-together look.

I also go for stainless steel appliances whenever possible. They look sleek and contemporary, and I'm betting that the stainless steel look, having been the standard in commercial kitchens for years, is going to be the mainstay in residential kitchen design for decades.

Ranges

The standard widths for ranges are 24 inches, 30 inches and 36 inches, and they generally come in two styles—freestanding and slide-in. Most kitchens are built for freestanding ranges. Slide-in models have no back, and the top edges slide over the countertops. These are easiest to put into a new kitchen or to add when you are replacing a countertop because they are designed to have a bit of countertop running behind them and a smaller break in the counter so that the range can fit snugly into the space with the top resting on the countertop. They do give the counter a sleek look. (If you are putting in a granite countertop with a standard stove, you may want to ask the granite supplier to give you a small piece of granite that can fit behind a slide-in model in case you opt for one later.) A third option is the separate range with built-in ovens—usually located in a wall at about waist height. The separate range top and oven setup, however, is usually a bit pricey.

Your other decision with regard to ranges and ovens is, of course, the fuel source. The trend these days is toward gas ranges—they provide more control over the level of heat, as they don't leave a hot element when turned off and can go from a small flame to a strong one almost instantly. (Ovens with electric heat, however, are considered preferable for baking. Dual-fuel ranges give you a gas stovetop and an electric oven but are usually considerably more expensive than a single-fuel range and are not likely to get you the best ROI). And while the fuel source is really a personal preference, keep in mind that switching from one to another usually requires other changes. If you are going from electric to gas, you will need to run a gas line if there isn't one in place (and this can be expensive). Electric and gas stoves require different types of electrical plugs, so these will need to be switched out. And finally, gas ranges need more powerful ventilation. In all likelihood, you will have to replace or provide a new range hood if you are moving from an electric to a gas range. All of that being said, a gas range is usually regarded by homebuyers as a higher-end item and will therefore bring greater value to your kitchen reno than an electric range. If possible, opt for gas.

Range Hoods

Range hoods vented to the exterior are a necessity if you have a gas stove, but they are an important addition to any kitchen. There are four standard types of range hoods: freestanding (ceiling-mount), surface-mount (under-cabinet or wall-mount), microwave hood and downdraft vents (which sit at the back of or flush with the top of the range top). They can be recirculating, charcoal-filtered or vented to the house exterior (this is ideal). While any of these types can be quite expensive, you don't want to cut corners on this part of your kitchen, because the range hood is really a safety element. The absence of a range hood—or the wrong type can have a big impact on the rest of your house. Without proper kitchen ventilation, ceilings can get stained, walls can be discoloured, drapes, carpets and upholstery can become impregnated with cooking smells, and kitchen cabinets can become warped from excess humidity. Worse, improper ventilation of a gas stove can pose health issues for those living in the house.

There are two things you need to consider when choosing a fan: the CFMs, or cubic feet per minute, of air circulated and the noise factor. In less expensive models, the higher the CFMs, the noisier the fan is. In more expensive units, better sound insulation and motors mean that the more powerful models are not as noisy as their cheaper cousins. It's always a balancing act deciding on how much air circulation and noise you can afford!

There are no regulations about the minimum CFMs you should have, but electric ranges usually need a hood with about 150 to 300 CFMs. To calculate the CFMs needed for gas ranges, take the total number of BTUs that all of the elements and the oven could produce, and then divide that number by 100. Keep in mind that you may want to bump that number up if you have the fan mounted very high above the cooktop or if the fan does not cover the entire cooktop area.

As I've said, ideally all of your appliances should match, but it's unlikely that your range hood is going to be manufactured by the same company as your fridge and stove. (Cyclone brand range hoods are my favourites, for example.) Just make sure that the look is compatible with your appliances—stainless steel with stainless appliances, white with white, and so on.

LIGHTING

Unless you are doing a complete kitchen reno, there is often not a lot you can do to update lighting in a kitchen. If you have a single ceiling-mount fixture, you can replace it with track lighting to spread the light out and direct it to an extent. See page 40 for more on kitchen lighting.

One final note: I haven't mentioned flooring as part of the basic upgrade because replacing or installing a floor is a renovation that belongs in the "full upgrade" section. Flooring should really extend under all cabinetry so that if cabinets are changed or moved in any way, you don't have a gap in the floor. And quick and inexpensive flooring options—press-and-stick tiles, for example—are going to look shabby after a very short time, so they are not worth the even minimal expense or labour.

Refacing

The next level of upgrading can include all of the improvements listed in the basic upgrade but also addresses tired or dated cabinets. Many people, when faced with kitchen cabinets they don't like, think their only recourse is to tear them all out and start again. But that can add more work, and more expense, than is actually necessary to get a whole new look. Refacing can totally transform the appearance of your cabinets—the design, wood variety, colour, detail—giving the effect of a complete kitchen reno, but at half the price of new cabinetry. And getting twice the bang for your buck means you can earn a 150 to 175 percent return on investment for this home improvement.

But there are some conditions your kitchen needs to meet to make this a viable option. First, the current kitchen layout has to work well. Next, the cabinets must be well fabricated, well mounted and in good shape.

This is not something, however, that you can do yourself. Refacing companies (this service is also offered by some big-box stores and traditional cabinetry businesses) will "reskin" the cabinet boxes with a laminate or wood veneer of your choosing. They will match this on the doors and can add crown moulding or a valance on the cupboards if you don't have one, or switch out ones that you don't like (see page 40 for more on mouldings and valances). New drawers and cabinet hardware (hinges, slides, silent drawer closures and so on) can be provided as well. You can also opt to have some cabinets replaced with drawer inserts if you'd like. And this is a quick job. All measurements can be done in less than a day, and a week or two later, when the doors are finished, the installation and completion can be done in a day.

In order to determine whether refacing is a viable option for you, inspect your current cabinets carefully. Look under the sink for swollen wood or fibreboard (this is where you usually see the first signs of deterioration). If you notice different pieces of plywood, this may be a sign that there have been efforts made to repair damaged cabinets. Make sure that none of the shelves are broken or loose. If all looks well maintained and in good working order, then refacing might be the option for you.

The base cabinets are solid wood and were in good shape, so they were easy to paint and reuse. Colour gives them a modern look.

Complete Kitchen Replacement

Sometimes, it makes sense to start from scratch. In many of the homes I've remodelled, the existing kitchen just wasn't serving its purpose. There might have been damaged or flimsy cabinets, a lack of cupboard space or an awkward layout. In these situations, it's great to reimagine the whole space and replace everything—from cabinets to appliances to floors— and reconsider the layout.

It's estimated that a total kitchen redo can bring a 75 to 100 percent return on investment. However, if you follow my advice, returns of more than 100 percent are not unreasonable! Here's what you need to do.

LAYOUT

The first thing to consider when you are doing a complete kitchen replacement is the layout. Perhaps the floor plan works well as is. But maybe there are ways to improve the work spaces, storage and traffic flow.

In the standard kitchen layout, the refrigerator, the stove and the sink form a "work triangle" that, in total, measures no more than 26 feet. Each arm of the triangle should be between four and nine feet. Ideally, an unbroken countertop of 36 inches would run between the sink and the refrigerator to create a food prep area. This design is meant to make cooking and working in the kitchen efficient and easy. It works best if there is as little traffic as possible cutting through the triangle and if islands do not cut into the triangular traffic flow too much. This way, cooks can move from sink to stove to fridge with as few steps and as little interruption as possible.

While the work triangle is a good rule of thumb, it is based on the idea of a moderately sized kitchen, with a single sink, a range, a fridge and one person at a time working in the space. A really large kitchen might have more than one triangle, and include two sinks (a prep sink and a larger wash area), a stovetop and wall ovens, and perhaps a bar fridge and a full-size refrigerator. Alternatively, in small kitchens, the triangle can be flattened out so that the fridge, sink and stove all run in a line along the same wall (a galley kitchen). If possible, the sink should be positioned in the middle, with 36 inches between the fridge and sink, and at least 15 inches between the sink and the range.

Another important factor in the kitchen layout is counter space. You should try to have 36 inches of counter space on one side of the main sink; at least 15 inches on the handle side or within reach of the fridge (or on either side for a side-by-side fridge); and 15 inches on one side of the range.

Just for You

When it comes to kitchens, there is no end to the bells and whistles you can add. Want a built-in wine cooler or fancy water filtration system? Then go for it! Just remember that those extras won't bring up the value of your house, so they are only worth it if you will get a lot of personal enjoyment from them.

(For more design guidelines, check out the National Kitchen and Bath Association: www.nkba.org).

People also tend to like to have the sink under a window—both for added light and for someplace to look while doing the dishes. But move your sink under a window only if you can do so without making the window smaller. Light is perhaps the most valuable asset in a kitchen—and natural light is as good as it gets. Don't sacrifice it if you don't have to.

As mentioned earlier, the kitchen has become the centre of the home. Because we spend so much time there, many people are opting for an open-concept design. Sometimes this means that the kitchen and dining room are combined to make a large space with a more informal eating area. Sometimes the kitchen opens into a main-floor family room. Either way, kitchen islands make a lot of sense in an open-concept kitchen design (as well as in any sizable kitchen)—they can serve as a place for people to sit for a meal, and they can provide storage space, which you need in an open-concept design because you have less wall cabinetry. Kitchen "peninsulas," in which base cabinetry continues (sometimes around a corner) but the upper portion of the wall is removed, can serve the same function as an island. Usually with a peninsula, the countertop extends farther out on one side of the cabinets to create a breakfast bar.

And finally, when planning your new kitchen layout, keep these tips in mind:

- place the dishwasher immediately adjacent to the sink;
- even if you are not putting in a dishwasher now, rough it in so you have the option in the future (this means providing a 24-inch cabinet close to the sink that can be swapped out for a dishwasher later);
- make sure no cabinet or appliance doors interfere with one another;
- ensure that open appliance doors don't get in the way of traffic flow;
- keep major traffic flow from intersecting the work triangles, if possible;
- maximize storage space in whatever ways you can;
- create a space for eating, if possible;
- try not to have appliances stick out past the base cabinet depth or to have tall structures blocking sightlines in the kitchen—keep a clean, open look.

The creative use of flat pack cabinetry can both maximize storage and space and give you a custom-kitchen look at a budget price. We double- and triple-stacked horizontal units with awning doors to create an eye-catching contemporary look that maximizes storage in a small kitchen.

CABINETS
Flat Pack Cabinetry

A complete kitchen reno will, of course, involve new cabinetry. But the days when every quality kitchen demanded custom cabinetry are over. I'm a big fan of "flat pack" or "knock-down" cabinetry—that is, standard kitchen cabinets offered by the big-box stores. Flat pack cabinets used to be frowned on by some, but the quality of many of these offerings has improved vastly over the last few years, and you can now get great-looking, well-made cabinets for a fraction of the price of a custom kitchen. These sorts of cabinets come in set heights, widths and depths, but can be combined in different configurations. You can even use the shallower (usually 12 inches) upper cabinets below the counter in tight places where the deeper lower cabinets (usually 24 inches) won't fit. In kitchens with really high ceilings, you can also stack upper cabinets one on top of another so that you fill the space. And because so many of the companies that offer this type of cabinetry also provide free online kitchen design programs, you can essentially build a custom kitchen for much less money.

With flat pack cabinetry, installation can be arranged through the store, or you can do it yourself. And this is where the wrinkle comes in: no matter how great the cabinets are, if they aren't properly assembled and installed, you may be in for some nasty surprises. Many do-it-yourselfers can be fooled by the simplicity of flat pack cabinets. But installing cabinetry is a bit more complicated than screwing the boxes together. It's essential that you know what is behind the wall you are mounting the cabinets on and that you locate all of the studs accurately. With plaster and lath walls, for example, it is easy to mistake a strip of lath for a stud—and screwing a cabinet into that tiny strip of wood instead of the two-by-four might mean the whole cabinet ends up at your feet once it is loaded with 100 pounds of dishes and cookware. So while you can save yourself some money installing cabinets yourself, it's important to take the time and care to do it right.

Using flat pack cabinetry is the most cost-effective way to do a complete kitchen replacement, and so it is also the best way to profit on this major level of renovation. Using flat pack cabinetry, you can expect a return in the order of 90 to 140 percent!

Custom Cabinetry

Despite the growing quality and popularity of flat pack cabinetry, custom cabinetry still accounts for 50 percent of the kitchen market, and if you have the budget for an upper-middle to higher-end kitchen, a custom cabinetry company can deliver the very best quality cabinets in just about any configuration you want. With custom cabinetry, you can get creative with the layout of your kitchen. You can change the height of your cabinets (especially useful if you have an old house with high ceilings); build in angled cabinets or shelves; customize cabinetry around range hoods; or put in features like wine racks, glass fronts or a fridge surround for a built-in look. You can opt for an integrated buffet or add toe plates to sections of cabinets so that they mimic freestanding furniture. You can also often maximize cabinet space by fitting cabinets into areas where standard-sized cabinets won't fit. And for a really unified look, you can have fronts made for your dishwasher and fridge doors so that they match the cabinet doors. Often, custom-kitchen builders can also provide drawer and cupboard hinges and slides with superior durability and strength. While flat pack cabinetry tends to use wood veneers, custom cabinetry can provide solid wood—in about any type or finish you want. And your choices for knobs and hardware are endless.

The beauty of a custom kitchen is that you can get *exactly* what you want instead of what is available with a preset product line. But when considering custom work, it's best to keep in mind the 5 to 10 percent rule. While the kitchen will be the most expensive room in the house no matter how you slice it, you don't want to go overboard here and build a kitchen that is really not appropriate to the value of your home—at least not if you want to maximize the value of the property. That being said, a custom kitchen may be what your property demands; just don't expect more than a 75 to 100 percent return on your investment due to the costs this kind of reno entails.

With either flat pack or custom cabinetry, as you pick out the elements, think about what you need to store and how you like to use your kitchen. For example, pots-and-pans drawers are an increasingly popular feature, but drawers in general are often a good way to make use of the under-counter space (you don't have to dig to the back of a two-foot cabinet to find things). Or if your family gravitates to the kitchen to do homework or work on their laptops, consider things like a built-in desk or study area.

LIGHTING

Lighting for a kitchen is unlike lighting in any other room of the house. Kitchens are indeed places to gather, eat and socialize, but they are also places where we work. Not only does your kitchen lighting have to serve these different needs, it must also highlight the quality of the room itself. Great lighting, in other words, not only increases the functionality of your

Well-designed lighting with different options (and controls) adds great value add to kitchen.

kitchen; it also promotes its value and can make a significant contribution to the return you get on a smart kitchen renovation. For those reasons, most kitchen design today features a variety of lighting types. The most pleasant is, of course, natural light, so do try to maximize window space (and don't cover up any windows!).

Pot Lights

The ideal lighting for a kitchen is provided by pot lights, but these need to be carefully planned. Each light should be 20 to 23 inches away from the perimeter walls of the kitchen, so that it shines onto countertops and is not blocked by upper cabinets and crown moulding. This is also ideal because lights spaced this way will not cast a shadow over your work surface when you are standing at the counter. Pot lights are sometimes available with halogen bulbs, but be careful with these if your ceiling is quite low—they can get very hot, and if they are a foot or less overhead, they may make you uncomfortable. If you do have a low ceiling, you may want to go with flush-mount lighting fixtures with fluorescent or compact fluorescent bulbs.

Valance Lighting

Your countertops are generally 25 inches deep, with 12 inches of that covered by an over-head cabinet, so overhead pot lights aren't going to be able to light your whole work space. This is why under-cabinet lights (hidden by a valance) are such a great idea. But you should have the valance lights wired in—cords hanging down from the cabinets and plugging into wall sockets ruin the clean, sophisticated look of a kitchen. Valance lighting works best with LED bulbs, as halogens generate too much heat. Fluorescents can work well too.

Pendant Lights

Pendant lights over an island or eating area can give the area definition and lend the whole kitchen a modern, sophisticated look. Just make sure that you have the ceiling height to accommodate them and that they hang high enough that they don't interfere with those working or sitting beneath them.

When hanging pendant lighting over an island, make sure you have enough ceiling height and space below to work.

Crown Moulding Lighting

Where there is a space above the crown moulding, I like to add small lights behind it. The lights reflect off the ceiling and add a subtle warmth and brightness to the kitchen.

Other Lighting Considerations

I like to make sure that the range hoods I pick have lights built into them. This is a great way to illuminate the stove work area. And I always try to get extra lighting over the main sink—even if there is a window over the wash area, you'll need the lights at night. But perhaps the most important thing about lighting in a kitchen is not to scrimp. Different lighting areas and options can be wired on separate switches, so you don't have to have all of the lights on at all times if you don't want to. In other words, you don't have to worry about "over-lighting." But having inadequate lighting can be a huge frustration, and if you are concerned about getting top dollar for your home when you sell, a well-lit kitchen will make the whole space look more appealing to prospective buyers.

FLOORING

A recent survey of residential real estate listings revealed that the most commonly used phrase was "hardwood throughout." Clearly, realtors have discovered that wood floors throughout a home are a huge selling feature (despite the fact that the Appraisal Institute of Canada reports an ROI of only 50 to 75 percent for new hardwood floors). And for a kitchen, tile and hardwood are certainly the most desirable. But these days, there are lots of other options to keep the costs in line and the returns high, including vinyl, linoleum, cork and laminates. When you are trying to choose, keep in mind that the flooring has to tie in with everything else—the cabinets, the countertops and the rest of the house. If the kitchen is part of an open-concept floor plan, then you need to consider how the flooring you choose for the kitchen will transition into the other spaces. Using only one type of flooring throughout (hardwood, for example) makes the space feel bigger and more open. And if you are doing a complete kitchen reno, make sure that the flooring goes down before the cabinets and that it stretches from wall to wall. That way, if you need to make a change or move a cabinet, you'll have the flooring in the newly opened space.

Tile

Tile is a great choice for kitchen floors. It comes in a huge variety of styles and colours, is essentially waterproof and is easy to clean. As with backsplash tiles, plain floor tiles can be laid in different designs (herringbone, brick, etc.) and may also incorporate decorative accent tiles amongst the solid ones. The only drawbacks to tile are that it can be unforgiving when a plate or a glass is dropped on it, and some people find standing on it for long periods to be hard on their backs and feet.

There are essentially three types of tile: porcelain, ceramic and natural stone. My favourite choice for kitchen floors is porcelain tile. I use it in about 90 percent of the kitchens I remodel. The great thing about quality porcelain is that it is the same colour throughout—if it chips, it's not as noticeable as a damaged ceramic tile, which usually has a coloured glaze covering its surface. But be careful when choosing porcelain tile. More and more manufacturers are selling porcelain tile that uses coloured glazes over white porcelain, which eliminates this advantage. That said, all porcelain tile is very durable. It is essentially the same material as

In an open-concept area, maintaining consistent flooring throughout contributes to the spacious feel. Here, hardwood in the kitchen is the perfect choice.

standard ceramic tile but denser, making it more resistant to cracking and staining. So while porcelain is a bit more expensive than ceramic, it holds up better in the long run. It's worth the investment, as far as I'm concerned.

Natural stones, like slate, marble and granite, are available as floor tiles. Slate has become so inexpensive that, in my opinion, it is being overused. As a result, while it is durable, slate doesn't really add the air of luxury that it once did. Natural slate, which has an uneven surface texture and a variegated colour, lends a very rustic look to a space. (And because the tile depth is uneven, your grout lines might end up being uneven as well.) Polished slate offers a more sophisticated, contemporary look. Marble and granite are also available as floor tiles—and in a wide variety of colours and some very attractive mosaic patterns. But when opting for granite and marble floor tiles, use caution. The inexpensive marble and granite types used for floor tiles can contain veins and inconsistencies that lead to cracking. This is of particular concern with larger tiles and when tiling large areas. And all natural stone floors need to be sealed immediately after they are installed, and again once or twice a year.

Hardwood

Years ago, hardwood was thought to be an impractical choice for kitchens. People were concerned with potential water damage. But how much water really ends up on a kitchen floor? And who doesn't clean up the occasional spill right away? The prefinished hardwood flooring available today is well sealed, durable and good-looking, making it perfectly suitable for kitchen use. But if you are really worried about moisture, you can opt for an engineered hardwood. Made with layers of wood covered with a wood veneer, engineered hardwood withstands changing moisture levels without expanding, contracting or twisting. And like solid hardwood, it can be refinished eventually, if necessary, although not as many times as solid hardwood.

Putting hardwood in a kitchen has the advantage of minimizing transitions from room to room if the rest of the house features hardwood as well (that is, as long as you choose matching hardwood). This is especially useful in an open-concept floor plan.

Laminates

Laminate flooring is made by applying what is essentially a photograph of wood, stone or tile over planks of particleboard, then covering this with a clear, durable coating. Laminate flooring is moderately priced and easy to install. It also is available in a wide range of looks—in just about any colour or grain of wood that you can imagine, as well as in stone and tile options. But the greatest problem with laminates is that if the top layer gets chipped or scuffed, the damage is really noticeable—and there is no way to fix it. Another drawback of laminates in a kitchen is that if you do have a leak, the particleboard swells very quickly, buckling the floor. Your only option then is to pull the planks out and replace them. For those reasons, I have never used tile-look laminates and have chosen wood-look laminates for a kitchen only if I am matching them with flooring in another room.

Vinyl, Linoleum and Cork

Vinyl, linoleum and cork flooring are all available in peel-and-stick tiles or sheets. But let me say right off the bat that I am not a fan of any peel-and-stick product. The adhesives in these products never really cures, so there is always the possibility that the tiles will move. Once they start slipping, it's a gong show—you just can't get them looking good again. And even if they haven't slipped, it is almost impossible to lay them tight enough that dirt doesn't collect in the sticky seams. So unless you are planning to sell your house the day after you install the tiles, this kind of flooring won't add any value to your home—and savvy buyers will offer a little less when they spot the product!

Vinyl

Glue-down sheet vinyl used to be a common type of flooring for kitchens. Many liked the cushiony feel. And it is waterproof and easy to clean. But sheet vinyl will scuff and scratch, and because it is so pliable, it will show any imperfection from the surface beneath it. You need to put sheet vinyl down over a new subfloor or use an epoxy skimming product over the existing floor to even everything out.

For those reasons, my preference, when going with a vinyl floor for the kitchen, is a product called Karndean. It's a solid vinyl plank flooring. The planks come three feet long and five inches wide and can be cut easily with a utility knife. A floor adhesive is trowelled over the existing floor, and once the planks are in place, this adhesive cures completely, so there is no movement in the floor. And unlike vinyl sheets or tiles, the colour of the vinyl is not limited to a top layer but goes right through the vinyl. This makes plank vinyl flooring exceptionally durable—and any nicks or cuts easily escape notice (which is why you often find these

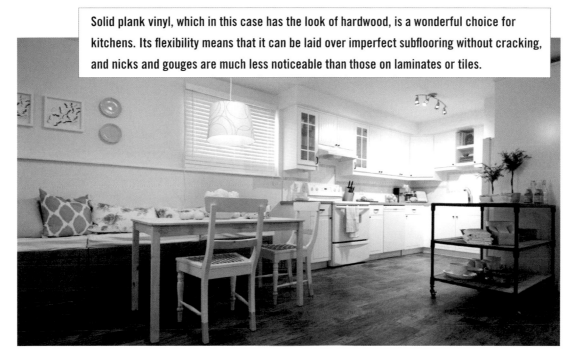

Solid plank vinyl, which in this case has the look of hardwood, is a wonderful choice for kitchens. Its flexibility means that it can be laid over imperfect subflooring without cracking, and nicks and gouges are much less noticeable than those on laminates or tiles.

kinds of floors in high-end hotels and stores). But the best thing about vinyl plank flooring is that it can go directly over concrete slabs—making it an ideal product for basement apartments, where you want the slimmest floor possible so that you lose as little ceiling height as possible. And like all vinyl, Karndean comes in an extensive variety of colours and patterns. The price point for this type of flooring is mid-range, and installation is easy to do yourself.

Linoleum

Linoleum was first introduced to the market in the late 19th century but has seen a revival in the last couple of decades. It is an environmentally friendly product made from cork and wood dust, combined with linseed oil. It's available in tiles and sheets. Like sheet vinyl flooring, it has to be applied over a perfectly flat surface. And like plank vinyl flooring, linoleum is solid all the way through, making nicks and scuffs almost unnoticeable. Marks and scrapes can even be fixed with a light sanding and resealing.

Cork

Cork flooring works well in kitchens because it is cushiony, keeping feet and backs comfortable, and because it's antibacterial. Because of its natural colours and pattern, it transitions nicely to other wood products. Since it is solid all the way through like plank vinyl and linoleum, cuts and dents aren't particularly noticeable and can be touched up like those in linoleum. Cork flooring comes in tiles or floating floor planks. Tiles need to be installed over a perfectly flat subfloor (just like vinyl or linoleum), but plank cork flooring is as easy to install as laminates or hardwood.

There's no doubt about it—improving your kitchen is a great way to raise the value of your home. And in many ways, keeping your kitchen updated is a necessity. Kitchens are so important to buyers that a space that looks dated, cramped, dingy or in bad repair can knock down your house's value in a big way. But there are so many elements to consider in a kitchen and so many choices that a kitchen reno can be a complicated and costly task. So before you start, really think about what you want, what you can afford and what is appropriate to your house. Check out decorating and design magazines and home reno shows for inspiration. Then research, shop and plan with this big picture in mind.

Kitchen Shopping Tip

There are probably more choices to be made during a kitchen reno than with any other home improvement job. What kind of flooring? Which cabinets? What type of faucet? What sorts of appliances? And on and on. Even if you have clear ideas about what you want, where do you find all of these things? One time-saving trick is to find a look you love in a home design magazine and then use the source guide at the back of the magazine or online to track down all of the elements instead of doing all the legwork yourself.

Small Touches That Add Up in the Kitchen

If you're on a limited budget, or even if you're not, here are simple ways to add value to your kitchen.

1) Use quality cabinet hardware

Dated or damaged hardware can make the whole kitchen feel that way. And since you're using knobs, pulls and handles all the time, invest in ones that feel solid and top quality. It's always a good rule of thumb to ensure that whatever you touch regularly in a house feels good.

2) Think about great lighting for work areas—day and night

Whether or not you have much natural light in your kitchen, plan lighting for all times of the day. If you have a window above your sink, washing dishes during the day isn't a problem, but at night you may need extra light.

3) Invest in a statement piece

If you can't afford the best of the best of everything, invest in one statement piece for your kitchen, such as a quality range hood, an island or a unique lighting fixture.

4) Add cabinet features

Display cabinets, glass doors and open shelving in some or all of your kitchen cabinetry are inexpensive options that add interest.

5) Add dimmer switches and a variety of lighting controls

One of the most affordable upgrades is adding dimmer switches to your kitchen to bump up your lighting options.

6) Change or add cabinet trim to your cabinets if you're repainting them

If you have flat-front cabinet doors, you can add trim to fake a shaker style. Dated-looking cabinets can also be refreshed with trim and paint.

7) Use quality taps and faucets

As with knobs and handles, you can actually feel the quality. You don't have to spend too much for good fixtures, but make sure they feel solid and work well.

Chapter 3

BATHROOMS

After the kitchen, the bathroom is the most important room in the house when it comes to improving your home's value. I've heard return on investment rates for bathroom renovations and upgrades that ranged anywhere from 60 to 100 percent. But why aim that low? If done wisely, a bathroom remodel can not only recoup your initial investment it can actually turn a tidy profit. In fact, I've installed bathrooms that I know have returned 150 to 200 percent on my investment. But to see this kind of result, you've got to get the reno right—aesthetically and technically. And you have to avoid mistakes. As far as I'm concerned, bathrooms are probably the worst places in the house to make a renovation error. With the quantity of water that flows through this room, a plumbing defect can severely damage not just the room itself but the entire house.

There are really only two levels of renos that can be done on a bathroom to get a great return on your investment. The basic and least costly is to keep the existing layout and lightly remodel, doing things like painting walls, replacing towel bars and replacing fixtures like lights, mirrors, toilets and vanities.

Your second option is to gut the bathroom and rearrange the layout. If the room has a horrible layout, this is the way to go. If the layout is functional, your return on investment will be greatest without changing fixture locations. The cost of permits and plumbers will eat into your profits if it's not done for better layout.

Replacing the fixtures will cost you a bit of money, but it's an easy DIY project. Anyone can change a toilet, as long as he or she can lift it. Standard toilet models are held down by only two bolts—that's it. So if your toilet is a bit dated, make a switch!

The Basic Upgrade

TOILETS

When choosing a new toilet, there aren't a whole lot of options for you to consider. If you really tried, you might be able to get your hands on something fancy. There are Japanese models (sometimes called "washlets") that feature built-in bidets, seat warmers, air dryers and other cleaning features (for you and for the toilet itself). There are even models that play music to relax the sitter and deodorize themselves after use. But this kind of high-tech toilet is really uncommon outside of Asia and certainly isn't going to get you anything other than a few comments and raised eyebrows when you sell your house. Put simply, in North America, no one is willing to pay extra for a toilet that responds to voice commands. All people really want is something that is clean and that works well. Ninety-nine percent

With a little design ingenuity, you can often add significant value to your home by squeezing a second or third bathroom into a tiny space. Here we were able to fit a three-piece bathroom under a staircase by installing a pocket door, putting the toilet at a right angle to the sink, placing the faucet at the side instead of at the back of the sink and using a double-hinged shower-stall door.

of toilets in this part of the world, in fact, are simply a bowl, a tank and a handle or button for flushing. The only big change here in the recent past is that the large tanks are gone in favour of water-efficient six-litre designs. Many of these now come with a dual flush system, so you can use even less than six litres for clearing liquid waste. The other minor variations include elongated bowls and seats, which give the fixture a higher-end look and are considerably more comfortable.

You can also opt for pressure-flush toilets, which work well in basements or areas below grade. The tanks hold water but also use the city water pressure to produce a more powerful flush with less water. These are not much more expensive than regular toilets, but they are noisy, so don't be alarmed!

The only other option you may have is the design of the toilet seat. If your toilet doesn't come with a seat, make sure that you choose one that matches the dimensions (width and length) of the bowl. And opt for one with a "quiet close" design if available. This feature costs a little bit more, but it prevents the seat from slamming down. Instead, once the seat and seat cover are moved past the completely open position, they slowly and quietly descend into place. It's a nice feature for everyone—but a great one for little boys!

SINKS AND VANITIES

Changing a sink or vanity can be a bit more work than swapping out a toilet because you have to disconnect the hot and cold water lines and the drain. And if the vanity is affixed to the wall, it might take a little work to remove it. But as far as improving the value of the bathroom, the vanity is a great place to focus—along with the mirror, it's the first thing you see in the bathroom. And there are a lot of different ways you can go with this particular fixture.

A sink can be a small, wall-hung fixture or set in an eight-foot-long vanity with multiple drawers. Pedestal and wall-hung sinks are good choices for powder rooms or small bathrooms where storage is not a concern. They will also give you the most accessibility in the room, as you can move around them fairly easily. A pedestal sink has the advantage of hiding most of the plumbing (and the pedestal provides support for the sink itself).

For most bathrooms, however, including upgraded powder rooms, a vanity with storage is the way to go.

Replacing a Toilet

Materials needed: new toilet, wax seal with gasket.
Tools needed: gloves, wrench or Channellock pliers, small hacksaw, scraper, rags.

The first thing you want to do before taking on this job is to get properly attired. Wear gloves and an old shirt that you are prepared to throw away if things get a bit messy. Next, take off the tank lid and put it aside. Then shut off the water line that runs to the toilet. If there isn't a shut-off valve on the toilet line, you will have to shut off the water for the whole house, and you should plan on adding a shut-off valve to the toilet when you are changing it. Once the water is off, flush the toilet until the tank is empty. There will be a little water left in the bowl. (You can try to plunge or scoop that out or try to empty the bowl by rocking it back and forth once the screws are loose so that the water empties into the drain after you have loosened the bolts. You may have to cut through any silicone sealant at the base of the toilet with a small knife first. You can also lift the toilet over a bucket or tub so that any remaining water drains there instead of onto the floor once you've got the bolts loose.)

Next, remove the bolt covers at the base of the toilet and, using a wrench or Channellock pliers, loosen the nuts that are underneath. If the nuts are rusted and you can't remove them, you can use a hacksaw and, sawing under the nut, cut the bolt top and nut off. If that doesn't work, get a hammer and smash the porcelain around the bolt. Make sure you are wearing safety glasses when you do this, and be careful when removing the shards of porcelain from under the bolt. Then slide the bolts out of the flange.

If there is caulking around the base of the toilet, cut through this with a small knife. Then rock the toilet carefully back and forth to break the wax seal under the base. When the toilet is free of the wax, lift it off and remove it. (You may need an extra set of hands for this.)

Once you've moved the toilet off the flange, put a crunched-up garbage bag or take-out coffee cup into the hole so that things don't fall down it and sewer gases don't rise up from it. You can buy a temporary cap for the hole, if you prefer. If the bolts are still in the flange, remove them.

Next, clean the remainder of the wax off the flange. You can use a trowel, a multi-tool or any type of scraper. Wipe the flange so that it is as clean as possible. If there is a rubber gasket on the flange, remove it and throw it away. Don't reuse it. Before you proceed any further, inspect the flange, making sure there aren't any cracks in it or rot around it from a previous leak. If you find a cracked or broken flange or rot in the floorboards, you might want to call in a skilled plumber or carpenter to fix this bigger problem.

If your toilet did not come preassembled, put it together following the manufacturer's instructions, but put the seat on later. Your new toilet will come with its own new bolts. Put these bolts into the flange where the old ones were. Usually, the flange will have two-sided holes for the bolts. Pass the bolt through the large side and then slide it into the smaller side to secure it.

You will need to buy a wax seal for under the base. I use wax seals with a gasket versus the ones without because the gasket helps funnel things into the drain better. If the flange is very low to the floor, you can get an extended wax seal. I will often opt for this even if the flange isn't low, just to be sure. Make sure the seal is at least room temperature before you proceed further. If it is cool and hard, you may want to warm it up in the sun for half an hour before you centre it on the flange. And remember to remove the cup or rag from the hole before you add the wax seal.

Now for the hard part: placing the toilet on the wax seal and flange. Sometimes this step requires two people. Lift and lower the toilet over the flange and seal, making sure the bolts come up through the bolt holes at the base of the toilet. Twist the toilet an inch in each direction (or a tenth of a turn), putting pressure on the toilet to squish the wax seal and get the base to touch the floor. If the base hits the floor with no resistance, you need to get a bigger wax seal or a higher flange. Put the washers and nuts on the bolts and tighten carefully. Make sure that the toilet hasn't shifted and is still secure, but don't overtighten the bolts, as this may crack the porcelain. You may have to cut off the top of the bolt with a small hacksaw, grinder or reciprocating saw so that the bolt covers will fit. Be careful not to chip or scratch the porcelain. Put the bolt covers on, and then attach the toilet seat using a slot-headed screwdriver. Use the nuts provided to secure the seat.

Now you are ready to hook up the water line, hand-tightening it to the bottom of the tank. Attach the flex line to the water line and turn on the water valve. Allow the tank to fill up and then flush. One final note about installing a toilet: if you check other DIY videos or resources, you may notice that many recommend that you finish the toilet installation by caulking around the base with silicone sealer. In fact, some building codes require this final step. I, however, try to avoid this caulking, for a couple of reasons. First, if you do get a small leak under the toilet, the sealant will prevent water from leaking onto your floor, so you'll never know it's there. This can mean that the floor hidden under your toilet stays wet and begins to rot. Second, if you need to replace the toilet at a later date, you are unlikely to get one with a base exactly the same size. Then you will be faced with having to get rid of the messy caulking line on the floor from the first toilet. The sealant may prevent sewer gases and critters from escaping from a poorly sealed toilet, but if you've installed the toilet properly, with a good wax seal, there should be no gaps that will allow this to happen.

The standard vanity is 24 inches wide and 18 to 24 inches deep. If you have the space, however, go for a vanity that is 36 inches or wider and 24 inches deep. This will provide plenty of counter space, more storage and room for a large sink. It will also accommodate a nice-sized mirror with vanity lighting above it.

If a 24-inch vanity is all you can get into your space, it might be difficult to find one with a drawer. If the vanity is going to be in your main bathroom, where storage is an important consideration, you should think about spending a little more on one designed so that plumbing is streamlined to make room for a drawer. It's worth the extra expense.

As far as height goes, the standard bathroom countertop is about 30 to 31 inches above the floor. In recent years, some cabinetmakers and builders have been offering heights between 33 and 35 inches to accommodate taller people. These taller cabinets can be back savers, but while you want to be comfortable in your own bathroom, don't steer too far from the standard heights. Chances are that taller homebuyers won't expect or even notice the higher cabinets, but shorter folks shopping for a new home sure will!

Most vanities have a 17-inch drop-in sink and a three-hole faucet. These standard vanities can be purchased preassembled from big-box stores for as little as $150. But there are lots of variations and upgrades to choose from if you want something a little different. Vanities with vessel sinks and glass or stainless trough sinks can give your bathroom a modern, even funky look. Some people are even turning small pieces of furniture into vanities. These can

Easy Bathroom Fixes

As I mentioned at the start of this chapter, making mistakes when upgrading the bathroom can be costly, so I advise caution when considering DIY projects here. Quick and easy bathroom DIYs include putting up towel bars or toilet paper holders. You may be capable of swapping out the bathroom vanity, but remember that you have to detach and reattach the hot and cold water lines properly so that you don't have any leaks. And if there is not a separate shut-off valve to the water lines under the sink, you will want to add one.

While DIY projects in the bathroom may be limited, changing your toilet is a relatively easy one. It may sound like a job better left to professionals, but as I mentioned earlier, the toilet is held down by only two bolts, so removing the old one and fitting a new one in its place really isn't that difficult.

be striking and really attractive—in other words, a great way to add value to your bathroom. (But as always, if you are concerned with ROI, keep everything within reason. A handblown glass vessel sink may be stunning, but you aren't going to get your money back on it unless your house is very high-end and very current.)

COUNTERTOPS

As far as countertops go, your choices are more or less the same as those for the kitchen (with the exception of wood or butcher block): laminate, tile, composites, engineered stone and natural stone. My choices for bathrooms tend to be laminate, granite or marble. While marble is a bit porous and prone to staining, you really don't have to worry about spills in a bathroom like you do in a kitchen. Probably the worst thing you are going to splash on the countertops is toothpaste, and that's not really a staining hazard. And marble gives a bathroom a soft, bright look.

To determine what sort of countertops will give you the best ROI for your bathroom, remember that the finishes in your home should complement the value of your home. In a pricey neighbourhood, laminate may be too low-end, as buyers may expect a more luxurious look; in a neighbourhood with modest home prices, few people are likely to pay more for imported Carrara marble.

FAUCETS

There are lots of choices here, both in look and in operation. While two-handled models come in many styles that complement traditional or retro decors (as well as contemporary styles, of course), there is a lot to be said for the one-handled, levered varieties. Whether you are brushing your teeth or shaving, being able to adjust the water temperature or turn the water on or off by simply swivelling one handle can be a nice convenience. But there are even newer technologies that take this convenience a step further. Some recent models offer "touch" operation—all you have to do is tap the faucet itself (no need to turn any handles) and it comes on. And you can even purchase faucets that have the same sort of motion-controlled operation that you find in some public bathrooms. The motion-controlled, or "touchless," faucets usually require you to choose a water temperature that you leave set from day to day, so this might not be a good choice for your main or ensuite bathroom. But for a powder room, where you don't usually need really hot or really cold water, it's very efficient.

The Complete Bathroom Reno

If you are going to replace everything, you can rethink your layout and your lighting, as well as your tub, shower and flooring options. It's a lot to take into account, but given that the bathroom is the second most expensive room in the house (and the most expensive by square foot), it's worth spending the time to maximize the value of this renovation.

BATHROOM LAYOUTS

The layout of the bathroom is of key importance because it's such a small room with so many elements. The most standard functional layout is a room five feet wide and eight feet deep that runs lengthwise, with the vanity being the first fixture you encounter upon entering. The door should swing away from the vanity, and light and fan switches should be immediately inside the door, on the same side of the room as the vanity. The best bang for your buck usually comes from a 24-inch vanity, but sizes can range up to 48 inches, depending on the size of the room. The toilet would come next. Ideally, there should be at least 32 inches, but no more than 36, between the vanity and the shower, with the toilet in between. (A standard toilet is set 12 inches from the back wall to the centre of the flange, with at least 16 inches on either side of the centre of the flange.) The shower or tub stretches across the back wall, going wall to wall and running perpendicular to the length of the room. And finally, there should be an electrical receptacle near the vanity, but it must be three feet from the faucet or on a side wall so that it doesn't interfere with the mirror. It also needs to be a ground fault circuit interrupter (GFCI) outlet—the kind with the TEST and RESET buttons.

There are lots of possible variations to this layout, depending on the size and shape of the room, but you can use this floor plan as a general guideline. You don't, for example, want to walk into the shower stall as soon as you walk into the bathroom, or have to squeeze between a sink and toilet to get to the bathtub.

A few other things to consider when planning your bathroom:

- Ideally, the tub would not be under a window, nor would a window be in a shower stall. But if you don't have a choice, make sure the window is vinyl, and not metal or wood, and continue the waterproof membrane that you are using in the shower stall right up to the window edges. You can also opt for a glass block window. These can't be opened, of course, but they have the advantage of being watertight and opaque if you choose ridged or pebbled glass blocks.

- It's increasingly popular, and therefore likely to be seen as value-adding, to have the toilet in a separate enclosure or the shower and toilet in their own section of the bathroom, if space permits. The more intimate the function of the fixture, the more privacy people like to build into its space. But you need a relatively large bathroom to accommodate this kind of layout.

- Another big selling feature in bathrooms is the Jack and Jill washroom that offers two vanities or a double sink in a spacious vanity. This kind of design works especially well in an ensuite bathroom off a master bedroom or a bathroom shared between two bedrooms.

- In powder rooms, the standard layout is to have the sink and vanity directly in front of you as you enter the room, with the toilet off to the side. Powder rooms are usually compact so that they don't eat into the floor space of surrounding rooms or hallways.

- In many modern bathroom designs, people are getting rid of the combined shower and tub setup. There's no doubt that a separate glass-panelled shower enclosure and freestanding tub look great, but you need to have the space for this arrangement. If you have a small home with limited storage space, and you'd have to eliminate a bathroom closet to make this plan work, you may want to think twice about it. More important, if you have only one bathtub in the house, don't take it out when doing a bathroom reno. If you are not a bath taker, it may be tempting to eliminate the tub in favour of a large shower enclosure, especially if you don't have the space for a tub and separate shower. But bathtubs are essential to families with small children, and a house with no bathtub, regardless of how stylish and luxurious the bathrooms, will appeal to fewer buyers than one with this feature.

- When you need to maximize the space in any bathroom, you can play with swing of door or sometimes put in a pocket or sliding door. You can also adjust the size and

entrance of the walk-in shower to save space, and you may want to have a double hinge on the shower door so it opens both in and out to help with flow. And you can make a bathroom look bigger by using glass-enclosed shower stalls and generously sized mirrors to give the space a bright, open look. Another little trick for maximizing space: if you are doing a complete bathroom reno, you can have custom-built wall cabinets or storage units recessed between the wall studs. This way, they can be deep without sticking out very far into the room itself. You can even do this in existing bathrooms (where you are not redoing the whole new bathroom)—just make sure you hire a reliable contractor to do the work so that you don't puncture water pipes or hit electrical wires when you are going through the wall.

SHOWERS AND TUBS

Showers and tubs are really the most important part of the bathroom to do right—the potential damage caused by improper installation is something you don't want to risk.

Tubs

Standard tubs are about five feet long. (Washrooms are often five feet wide, so the tub fits perfectly across the back of the room stud to stud.) But you can get shorter and longer tubs, in all sorts of shapes. Tubs can be the standard drop-in style (with a skirt on one side), deck-mount (no skirt at all) or freestanding. The prices range from as little as $150 to $5,000 or more. I have used all kinds of tubs, but given that return on investment (whether on a rental unit or on a property resale) is always at the front of my mind, I haven't splurged on those really expensive tubs.

With the standard drop-in tubs, most people opt for the acrylic and fibreglass models these days. The older-style enamelled-porcelain-over-steel fabrications are cold and prone to chipping and can look a bit dated. When you purchase a drop-in tub, you need to know whether the faucets will be on the left or right as you look at the skirted side, and you need to install these tubs within a three-wall framed-out section of a bathroom.

Deck-mount tubs, by contrast, are simply dropped into a platform that can be any width and length, and they work very well in bathrooms that are wider than five feet, as you don't

A spa-like feel can be created with a few special design features in the shower area. Here, a build-in bench as well as frameless glass doors and walls give this shower a high-end look.

need walls to contain them. You can tile around them and up the side walls to provide a polished look. Deck-mount models also work well if you want a whirlpool tub, as you can add a removable panel on one of the sides so that you can easily get to the mechanics. But keep in mind, if you are tempted by a whirlpool drop-in or deck-mount tub, that they are more expensive and all the moving parts can be prone to failure. Whirlpool tubs also require more cleaning and maintenance to avoid mould buildup in the jets. For that reason, I don't recommend them for income properties. This is a "just for you" purchase—unless you install a very high-end model, you aren't likely to get any return on investment.

Freestanding vessel tubs can be elegant and dramatic. In a large bathroom, they can also be a design focal point. These days, there is a huge selection of fibreglass and acrylic tubs, but old-fashioned clawfoot tubs, while expensive, are still popular. But since they are made of enamelled cast iron, they are also the heaviest.

When selecting a tub (especially a deck-mount tub), avoid anything really oversized, unless you have another bathtub in the house and you have planned for the demands of a big tub. A very large tub can take forever to fill and can quickly empty your hot water tank. In fact, I heard of one family who only had one tub—and it was an oversized soaker. They also had very low water flow in the house. When they wanted to bathe the kids before bed, they would start the water running just as everyone was sitting down to supper. By the time the kids had eaten and the dishes had been cleared, the tub was finally ready! That's an extreme situation, but because of the capacity of a large tub, I recommend that you match it with a larger water line and a faucet and valve designed to maximize water flow.

If you have an old gem on your hands, like an antique clawfoot tub, re-enamelling might be an option.

Any tub you choose, like all of your other bathroom fixtures, should be white. After all, you can jazz up the tub or shower area with interesting tiles.

Showers

If the shower is not going to be part of the bathtub and its surround, the most inexpensive way to go is to install a prefab kit. These kits are most often designed to go into a relatively tight corner, with acrylic side and back panels and a glass door. (The "neo-angle" models have five sides: two acrylic corner walls, and a three-sided front that is composed of two angled glass panels on either side of a glass door). While cheap, cheerful and compact, there are drawbacks to these kit shower stalls. The hardest part is lining up the drain location. The next challenge is putting the whole thing together properly. There are a lot of screws and a lot of seams, and if the assembling and caulking aren't done accurately, the stalls tend to leak. In the rental properties I've purchased, I've pulled out about 50 or 60 of these prefab showers, and not one of them has been put together properly. If you do choose to put in a kit shower stall, go for a mid- to high-price unit, which will run you about $1,000 or $2,000. Anything cheaper is likely to be of poor quality and prone to leaks. And when you do assemble the kit, keep in mind that you should generally be caulking outside seams, not interior seams, so that water runs back into the system and not out of it.

Frankly, despite the economies of the kit showers, I prefer the Schluter shower systems. The Schluter system uses a variety of components to build custom shower stalls of any size or configuration (even wall-less showers with floors that slope to the drain). Schluter gives you a large selection of base styles made out of foam, which you can cut to accommodate your space. But the key to the Schluter system is the Kerdi waterproof membrane. This membrane is mortared to the foam base and then extended up the curb and the shower walls, which are built with waterproof Kerdi board. The Kerdi board can also be used to build in benches, seats or shelves. After all of the board is covered by membrane, the stall is finished by tiling on top of it. These steps create a fully waterproof and vapourproof shower. The stall can be closed off with a curtain, but I prefer using custom glass doors. Glass ups the ante as far as sophistication and quality go—and a door makes the shower splash-proof. You can go for framed doors or frameless, but I usually opt for the frameless styles. They are more expensive, but they involve fewer pieces, require less caulking and provide less chance for leakage and mould, as the water all runs back into the stall instead of stealing into crevices of the frame. In other words, frameless shower doors are going to last longer and stay looking good for longer, so despite the added initial expense, they are likely to give you a better return on your bathroom investment in the long run.

The older, traditional way to build a custom shower stall is what is often referred to as the "basket system." The floor is built to flow towards the drain. A large rubber membrane is installed over the floor, tying into the drain. The membrane is then extended six to eight

A waterproof membrane protects against mould.

inches up the wall to create a waterproof basket at the base of the shower. The membrane is secured to the cement board walls, and then the entire stall is tiled. The problem with this system is that leaks tend to happen through the tiles and into the upper walls—making the rubber basket ineffective. This is why I don't recommend this method for shower stalls.

There are a number of other ways to build showers (although, as I said, I think the Schluter system is the superior one), but the cardinal rule for any shower or tub area is that no organic material can be used for the enclosure itself. That means no wood, plywood, lumber, plaster, drywall or even greenboard. I've seen plenty of mould and mildew growing in the purported mould- and mildew-resistant stuff, and when greenboard gets wet, it crumbles. If any of these materials are used in a shower and you get a leak, mould will flourish.

If you install something other than the Schluter system—there are all kinds of tub and shower systems out there—just make sure that whatever you are using is manufactured by a reputable company with a history in the business. And choose products that have a 20- to 25-year warranty.

When installing a custom shower stall, I think it's a great idea to add a bench or seat. It's easy (just frame it out in your waterproof materials and tile over it) and doesn't add much to the expense, but it definitely adds value. It may appeal to older buyers, but people of all ages tend to like the spa-like feel it gives the bathroom. Keep in mind that any curb or seat in a walk-in shower has to have a 2 to 5 percent slope back into the shower.

Shower Valves

The shower valve and faucet are key elements in a bathroom. They should match the sink faucets, but there are many other considerations outside of aesthetic ones.

Most valves today come with one of two ways to keep hot and cold water balanced so that a relatively consistent water temperature is maintained—pressure-balanced valves and thermostatic valves. Pressure-balanced valves sense the change in water flow of the hot and cold streams. If, for example, the cold-water pressure drops suddenly because someone flushes a toilet, the valve reduces the flow of the hot water in the shower line to compensate. These valves do not, however, measure actual temperatures, and the temperature of the water must be chosen (by adjusting the lever) each time you run the water. Thermostatic valves include a thermostat that measures the water temperature and adjusts the flow of hot and cold water to maintain the temperature chosen. Thermostatic valves will usually have two levers. The first lever controls the actual water temperature and maintains its consistency and accuracy with a thermostat. The second lever controls the flow of water. The two-lever system may be a little more confusing, but these valves measure actual temperature and can therefore be more accurate. The temperature lever may be left at a certain setting to ensure consistent water temperature every time you re-enter the shower.

Both valves work well and add the same amount of value. It may be more of a personal choice as to which one is more suitable for you.

Most new valves feature one of these two options, but if you live in an older home, you may have original plumbing without these safeguards. If so, it's not a bad idea to replace the outdated valve. While this update may be done primarily for your own comfort and safety, and will not immediately give you a return on investment, remember that improving the value of your home depends not only on in-demand renos and regular maintenance but also on ongoing quality improvements.

Most newer single-handled shower valves also have an internal temperature adjustment that prevents really hot water from flowing through the shower (in essence, it's a device that prevents you from turning the handle to hot water–only position). If the hot-water temperature in the rest of the house is fine, but the shower is tepid or seems to run out of hot water quickly, you can adjust this to allow for a higher hot water flow. (You will need to check the manufacturer's instructions first.)

As far as showerheads and faucets go, if return on your investment is what you are worried about, you shouldn't go too fancy. These days, spa showers are cropping up in all sorts of bathroom renos—whether they include a huge rain showerhead or multiple shower jets in the stall walls as well as overhead. But these are expensive and complicated to install. Some even need their own water lines to accommodate the amount of water they are going to be spouting out. Most homes simply aren't going to see any return on investment from this level of upgrade. The exceptions will be very high-end properties, where a spa bathroom or luxury ensuite can be used as a selling point. Typically these showers need to be built from scratch.

But there are less pricey upgrades that are worth making in all bathrooms. Every shower should feature a low-flow showerhead. This type of head raises the water pressure of the water coming out without increasing the water flow. It feels as if a huge volume of water is splashing down on you—but it isn't.

I also like to add a tub spout in any shower-only stall (in a combined tub and shower enclosure, these are standard). The toe tester faucet allows you to turn on the water and adjust the temperature by checking the water as it flows from a tap near your feet before you turn on the showerhead itself. It can save you from nasty shocks.

When adding or replacing showerheads, I like to keep the spouts about seven feet high. The showerhead will drop down six inches with the elbow so that it reaches the average person, but isn't so low that most people can't get under it. (I've seen a lot of showerheads that have been installed too low.) If you are concerned about setting the showerhead at the appropriate height for a variety of people (which might be the case in families with children, for example), you might want to go with a handheld shower nozzle that slides up and down a pole attached to the wall. Adding this kind of showerhead doesn't require any demolition—you simply mount the post to the wall and tie the shower hose into the existing valve.

Tiling Shower Stalls and Bath Surrounds

Tiling in a bathroom not only protects walls from moisture and provides an easy-to-clean surface; it also can be a significant design feature. Since the square footage of most bathrooms is relatively small, I'll often raise my budget for tiles. Higher-end tiles, borders, accent tiles and floor inlays add an element of luxury that really raises the calibre of the space. And I always finish any exposed tile sides (like with a tub or surround) with an edge trim— a clean metal edging that finishes off the look.

The grout between the tiles is functional, of course, but it can also figure into the design. In some instances, you will want the grout to be close in colour to your tiles—white grout with white marble tiles, for example, always looks great. But there are other times when you can use a darker, lighter or contrasting grout colour to define the tiles and make them pop.

There are two types of grout: sanded and non-sanded. The size of the spacing between the tiles dictates which you use. Unsanded grout is only used for spacing less than one-eighth of an inch. When using natural stone or porous tiles, you will need to seal the tiles before they are grouted. (Otherwise, any grout that gets on the unsealed stone will be impossible to remove.) No matter what tile you choose for your shower or tub surround, be sure you have a moisture membrane behind it and a non-organic wall covering (like cement board) to ensure your work lasts and that any moisture that does find its way through the tiles doesn't cause any damage.

While I can't help giving advice about tiling (don't, for example, mix your grout too wet or it will shrink), I do hesitate to provide too much DIY guidance because, when it comes to renovations, tiling is at the top of my list of things you should have done by a professional. You can play around with drywall or laying hardwood or laminates—it's not so hard to correct your mistakes. But tiling needs real patience, and if you don't have a lot of experience, you won't get the spacing right or the tiles level. And even if you have done a bit of tiling before, different tile sizes lie differently. You are also likely to struggle with small transitions in walls, cutting around toilets or planning a tile layout that avoids partial tiles along the edges of the room. And while very few renos get completed without a few flaws and mishaps, tiling mistakes are really noticeable.

LIGHTING

If good lighting is essential in a kitchen, it is every bit as important in a bathroom. The wrong lighting here—which usually means too little lighting—is a real pain (and the frequent cause of nicked chins, poorly applied mascara and general frustration). You need to provide some light above the vanity, between the mirror and the edge of the vanity, where people will be standing—if the only lighting comes from behind a person standing in front of the mirror, it will be almost useless. You should also add lighting in other areas of the bathroom. (A good rule of thumb is to light the bathroom to avoid casting shadows in any part of it.) The vanity light source should be about seven feet high. Your vanity mirror, therefore, will have to be no higher than six feet above the floor, or be able to have lighting mounted within it or to the side of it. Wall-to-wall mirrors can have holes drilled in them for mounting light fixtures. A narrow mirror may allow wall sconces or other fixtures to be mounted to either side of it but still close enough to the centre of the vanity to be of use. If using pot lights in the bathroom, plan their placement carefully. Those in the ceiling above the vanity must be close enough to the wall that they are not positioned directly over you as you are standing in front of a sink. If they are overhead, they will cast shadows on your face, which makes even the most attractive person look like the walking dead. And any light that is too directional is going to cause problems—you want fixtures that are going to flood your face with even light.

And finally, avoid fluorescent lighting in a bathroom. The buzzing can be annoying, and the bluish light can be hard on your eyes.

Like in the kitchen, a variety of lighting options (with controls) is an important value add.

BATHROOM FANS

The fan in a bathroom is something no one will notice immediately, but it's a very important element in adding value to your property. Moisture is the number one enemy in your home. It will damage the structure, produce mould and rot, accelerate the decomposition of materials and attract critters (termites and carpenter ants like wet wood). And the bathroom is likely to be the primary source of moisture in your home. For that reason, getting a good-quality bathroom fan should not be overlooked.

There are two components of a fan that make all the difference. The CFM number (cubic feet per minute) tells you how much air the fan can circulate. A bathroom fan needs to be powerful enough to replace all the air in the room about eight times every hour. You must calculate the size of the bathroom in cubic feet and then purchase a fan with the appropriate CFM number. Here is how you calculate what size fan your bathroom requires: figure out the volume of the bathroom by multiplying length by width by height and dividing that number by 7.5 (if you need to replace the air in your bathroom eight times per hour, that equals every 7.5 minutes). This calculation will give you the proper CFM requirements for the room. Round up to the next standard fan model to be safe.

The sones rating of a fan—a number from zero to five—indicates the noise factor of the unit (the lower the number, the quieter the fan). Fans with the highest CFMs and the lowest sones factor will be the most expensive. But generally, bathroom fans range in price from $75 to $300. Given all of the other expenses in the bathroom, this is not a lot of money, and your best ROI will be achieved if you purchase the most appropriate fan for the room. It's also worth paying the higher price for a quiet fan if the bathroom is directly below a bedroom or other living area where the noise will be very noticeable.

One last note about fans: even the best-quality fan isn't going to be worth the expense if you don't use it. Some people like to have the fan tied directly to the light switch so that when someone turns on the light to use the bathroom, the fan is automatically activated. But if you are going that route, you have to be comfortable turning on the light even if the bathroom is well lit by natural light during the day, or for a period of time after you've left the room to clear the moisture from a shower or bath. For those reasons, some people put the bathroom fan on a timer. This way, they can leave it on when they turn the lights off and leave the bathroom, knowing it will go off after an appropriate amount of time. If you do have the fan on a separate switch from the light, try to keep the switches close so that the fan is not forgotten.

FLOORING

As with kitchens, you have a number of choices for bathroom floors: vinyl plank flooring, sheet vinyl and linoleum, natural stone, and porcelain or ceramic tile. While hardwood works well in the kitchen, there is just too much water running through a bathroom to make wood (whether it's engineered or solid) or even laminates (which have a particle-board base) practical choices. If any of these get soaked, they will heave and buckle and need to be completely replaced. And while many people favour marble for a bathroom, I don't like using a porous stone like this for the floors (although I don't mind it for walls). Marble tends to crack and chip easily at the corners, so you lose a lot of the stone while installing, driving your costs up. Unless marble has been thoroughly sealed for a bathroom, it takes a lot of maintenance. And it needs to be laid on a perfectly level, completely movement-free subfloor to avoiding cracking along the veins. In 95 percent of the bathrooms I do, I use ceramic or porcelain tile, and usually stick with standard floor tiles, as long as they don't have a slippery surface. (See page 44 for more on tiling.) In bathrooms where I can't properly level the floor for tiling (perhaps because I don't want to lose height in a basement), I opt for vinyl plank flooring.

For those considering carpet in a bathroom, see "Don't Do It!" on the next page.

Don't Do It!

The person who first carpeted a bathroom deserves the award for worst idea ever. No matter how tidy the room, no matter how careful you are, even if the bathroom is never used, the first thing most people think when they see a piece of carpet around a toilet is "germs." (Well, okay, maybe "germs" is a euphemism, but I don't think I need to spell out where these germs might come from.) So whatever you do, don't put carpet in a bathroom. And if there is carpet already there, rip it out—quickly. And while we are talking about things on the bathroom floor, avoid those little rugs that go around the base of the toilet. I know they can be washed, but they still evoke the same associations as bathroom carpeting.

If the bathroom floor can be a pitfall, so too can the most important piece of furniture in that room: the toilet. Let's be honest: no one ever bought a house because they liked the type of toilet it had. But many people might have decided not to make an offer, or lowballed the price, because they hated the bathroom. If carpeting is my first pet peeve in a bathroom, nonstandard toilets are my second. White bathroom fixtures are always the way to go. You may find that peacock blue or lavender toilet amusingly retro, but most homebuyers are just going to think "old" (or ugly). Even off-white bathroom fixtures tend to look dated. If you want colour in your bathroom, keep it on the walls. And stay away from toilet-seat modifications. Cushioned or wooden seats, and even those plush seat covers, are aesthetically questionable at best and hygienically dubious at worst. And a final word about toilets: don't put those blue pucks in the bowl, or the coloured liquid in the tank. Toilet cleaning should happen off-camera—most homebuyers don't want to be confronted with blue water or pungent cleansers, which oddly enough always seem to suggest a lack of cleanliness, rather than the opposite.

And finally, my last bathroom warning: bathrooms are oddly personal spaces. Every competent real estate agent is going to tell you that the best way to show a home is to depersonalize it. And this is especially true of the bathroom. Avoid a lot of artwork or decoration or, worse yet, whimsical signs in the bathroom. Keep this space clear, clean and minimalistic if you want your bathroom to be an asset rather than a liability when it comes to home value.

Heated Floors

Heated floors in a bathroom are becoming increasingly popular, and for good reason. Not only do they spare you from stepping out of the shower onto glacially cold floor tiles in the middle of winter, they also provide a nice source of ambient heat in the bathroom—particularly useful in bathrooms that are in cold spots like above a garage, in a corner of the house, or below ground level. While heated floors are nice to have, however, they don't really serve up a good return on investment, unless they are in a bathroom that actually lacks a heat source. In this case, they can transform a bathroom that is a bit of a liability into a quality space in the home, delivering a decent ROI.

To heat the floors, you can run radiant lines through your floor if you have the room, or go for an electric coil mat. A low-profile option is great for making the most of the height of the room or putting heated floors into an existing space. With retrofits, you don't want to raise the level of the floor so that people have to "step up" into the bathroom. When you choose a floor mat, it is essential that you choose the appropriate size for the room or have a mat custom made. This is important because you want to heat as much of the floor as possible. Bathrooms are usually awkward spaces with fixtures to work around, so getting a mat custom made will ensure every nook and cranny is heated.

If you are going to add a heated floor to your bathroom, you have to exercise real caution with the installation. It's best to get someone with experience to put in the system. And before covering the heating elements in any way, the installer needs to perform a resistance test that ensures that the system is working properly and none of the mechanics have been compromised. Once the heating is functioning, the only thing that can go wrong is with the thermostat. But if you skip the resistance test and discover issues after the rest of the flooring is in, your only option is to tear the floor out and start again.

After tiling over the heating system, make sure that you don't turn it on for at least seven to 10 days. It takes that long for the glue and the grout around the tile to dry naturally. If the floor heat is turned on before everything has cured, the grout will crack or the glue may not set properly.

A Great Little Value Adder: Heated Towel Racks

A heated towel rack is something you might think was a little extra that wouldn't give you a lot of return on investment. But you'd be wrong!

I've installed about 30 or 40 heated towel racks in the bathrooms I've done, and people just love them. In fact, the heated towel often becomes a big selling point in a rental property or even a house.

On top of giving the bathroom a great sense of luxury, heated towel racks can also serve a practical purpose. Many existing bathrooms don't have a heat source. But even if you are doing a complete reno or adding a new bathroom, you may not be able to build a heat source in. In houses without forced air, there may not be room for a radiator. If there are height issues in the bathroom (in a basement, for example), you may not be able to install in-floor heating. In those situations, a heated towel rack is a great way to warm up the bathroom. And even in bathrooms with a heat source, a heated towel rack can keep the bathroom really cozy by making it a bit warmer than the surrounding rooms.

Heated towel racks are not cheap. But in one of the most expensive rooms per square foot in the house, a heated towel rack gives you a big bang for your buck and is an easy way to add value to your home.

Small Touches That Add Up in the Bathroom

If you're on a limited budget, or even if you're not, here are simple ways to add value to your bathroom.

1) Pick frameless glass shower doors

It's an easy way to add a luxurious and spa-like look to your bathroom.

2) Offer a variety of lighting choices and controls

Lighting pays off in a bathroom. A good rule of thumb is to not leave shadows anywhere and to have separate light switches, including a dimmer switch, for flexibility.

3) Invest in quality taps and faucets

Anything you touch and use regularly in a house should feel solid and work well. You don't have to spend too much for quality fixtures.

4) Pay attention to your bathroom vanities

A vanity doesn't need to be expensive, and it can work as a design-forward statement piece that creates interest in the bathroom. Also, a vanity can be swapped out easily later.

5) Think long-term for your fixtures

Quality toilets, tubs, sinks and fixtures last longer, and a classic design never goes out of style.

Chapter 4

OTHER INTERIOR RENOVATIONS

Living and Dining Rooms

The main living space in houses used to be designed and built in a very compartmentalized way: a separate kitchen, dining room and living room. Life, however, has changed. We don't expect to have one person in the kitchen preparing food, then serving everyone in a separate dining room, after which the group "retires" to the living room. Today, most of us live in a home where everyone cooks at one point or another. We are often putting meals together on the fly or watching TV while we do it. We like to spend time with our family or guests while in the kitchen—while Dad prepares dinner, the kids are doing their homework at the kitchen table; or while a couple cooks, their dinner-party guests keep them company at the breakfast bar.

These days, builders usually acknowledge this kind of lifestyle by including an eat-in kitchen that opens into a main-floor family room in new houses. But in older homes, opening up the main floor to accommodate an open-concept kitchen, dining and living space is a great way to improve the value of your home.

Opening your main floor to the kitchen is a huge bonus. Our appliances are so much bigger than they used to be, and we have so many more of them, that they often don't fit nicely into a compartmentalized space. But even though most people want an open-concept main floor, they also like to define the spaces within the area. Flow can be improved by removing walls and continuing the same flooring throughout the space. But separate lighting, ceiling divisions, furniture layout and even different colours for walls give an open-concept space delineation and visual interest.

I do have one caveat about the open-concept renovation: if you have to remove any structural or supporting walls, this sort of renovation can get pretty expensive, as other support must be built in to replace the load-bearing walls. So it's a great improvement to make if you are doing a full kitchen reno or other major renovations where this level of work can be a continuation of the rest of the remodelling. But if all you want to do is open up the living room and dining room areas, this may not be a project that will get you a decent return on investment, particularly if the rooms are already a good size and the existing floor plan is not tightly compartmentalized.

On the main floor, there are also quick ways to give your home a higher-end look without spending much money. Traditional carpenter-fashioned wainscotting with large panels tends to cost a lot of money. But faux wall panels made with applied moulding with a chair rail above will give you a very similar look without the high cost (see Interior DIYs below). Crown mouldings, however, while a nice touch, won't add value, except in more expensive homes. And you should only add them in larger rooms with higher ceilings, as they can be overpowering in smaller spaces.

LIGHTING

As mentioned earlier, lighting can be used to define and separate areas of your main floor living space. And even separated kitchen, dining and living rooms tend to use different lighting options. Pot lights are great in a kitchen. I think a dining room area looks best lit with a pendant light. Some living rooms opt not to have ceiling lighting at all, but instead make use of table lights, floor lights or even wall sconces (which are most attractive if wired into the wall). You can also wire plugs and fixtures like sconces so that they can all be turned on at the same switch. Pot lights can also be used in the living room to accent the room. And, of course, lots of windows are a fantastic way to light your main-floor living space. Remember, updated lighting and well-lit spaces make a home feel more valuable, and since changing or

In the living room too, adding light fixtures (and choices) will likely get you back as much or more than you spend.

adding light fixtures is a relatively inexpensive and easy job, you are likely to get back as much or more than you spend.

Another great way to create attractive main-floor space is to make sure that every room or "area" has one defining feature. That might be a wall painted a different colour (an accent wall), applied moulding, a coffered ceiling, wallpaper or a fireplace. The key is to keep it to one feature per space for maximum impact. Adding more design features just diminishes the effect of each of the other features.

The right lighting can really make a room. Here, a mixture of different types of lighting creates a bright, airy space that makes you completely forget this is a basement. Overhead pot lights are complemented with attractive ceiling fixtures and pendant lights. Accent, task and decorative lighting provide brightness at different heights throughout the space. I bet you didn't notice that there are no windows in the space at all!

FIREPLACES

If you have a wood fireplace, great—because you can't add one to an existing home. You can, however, often add a gas fireplace (as long as there is a way to vent it to the outdoors) or an electric fireplace. But while fireplaces are great design features for a room, they don't add value to your home—other than aesthetically and in the personal enjoyment they may give you.

Front Entrances

Freshening up or improving a front entranceway isn't likely to improve the value of your home in a significant way, but like the exterior entranceway of your home, if the area is bright and inviting, it sets the stage for the rest of the house and can help hook homebuyers or just make your home more attractive to both family and guests. And part of making an entrance seem inviting is making sure it doesn't look like a rummage sale of shoes, bags and outerwear. If you have a closet, think about installing a closet organizer so that storage space is maximized and easy to use. If you don't have a closet, you might want to create some storage with hooks, a coat rack or a small wardrobe. An attractive bench with storage can also be used to stash shoes, hats, bags and gloves. It also serves as a convenient place to put on your boots.

The other item to pay attention to in the entranceway is the light fixture. Swapping out a light fixture is a quick, easy way to spruce up the space. A good light will also help brighten the area, but I like to put entrance lights on a dimmer switch so that I can use low light when I want a subtle effect.

An entranceway is also a good place to use quality flooring to make a high-calibre impression. The design of your home may not allow it, but if you have a separate, self-contained entrance area, splurge on quality tiles. As in other areas, you may arrange plain tiles to create herringbone or zigzag patterns, or you may choose tiles that have some texture or visual interest of their own.

And finally, entrances can obviously be high-traffic areas, so pay attention to the condition of the paint. This may be an area where you want to paint a bit more often than you would, say, a bedroom. Remember that light colours tend to make a room look bigger—a good thing to keep in mind to make the most of a small entranceway.

The front entrance to your house matters too. This inexpensive re-make included a closet, new flooring, a light fixture and seating.

Interior DIY Projects

There are a number of simple do-it-yourself projects for hallways and living rooms, dining rooms and bedrooms. Painting is an obvious DIY project. You can also update lighting fixtures, hang curtain rods, change your home thermostat or change door hardware (see page 92). Closet organizers and shelves are other improvements that may be easy for you to tackle on your own. Flooring is a little more challenging, although those with strong DIY skills might want to lay prefinished hardwood or laminate floors.

My favourite easy and inexpensive DIY project for the living room or dining room? Applied moulding or faux wall panels.

A Great Value Adder: Applied Mouldings or Faux Wall Panels

Materials needed: chair rail, applied moulding, carpenter's glue, brad nails, caulking and paint.
Tools needed: tape measure, pencil, level, square, mitre saw, nail gun and caulking gun.

The first thing you need to do is measure the height and width of the wall on which you want to add the panels. Then decide on the number and height of the boxes you want, the space around all sides of the boxes (this is typically between four and eight inches) and the height of the chair rail that will run above the panels. These decisions will be determined by the space you have, the ceiling height, the placement of receptacles and switches on the wall, and the look you would like to achieve. Tall panels draw the eye up and work well in rooms with very high ceilings. Low panels (which start a little more than halfway down the wall) work well with moderate ceiling heights and in smaller rooms. Next, measure the total length of the wall, and subtract the total of all the spaces at the sides of the panels, including the spaces in between the panels. Subtract the spacing measurement from the total length, and then take the remainder and divide by the number of boxes you will have. This will give you the width of each box.

Using a pencil or chalk, level, square and measuring tape, make a few small pencil marks on the wall to help you align the chair rail and the tops and bottoms of the panels. Cut the chair rail to the appropriate length. With the mitre saw, cut the moulding pieces to appropriate length, with cuts at 45 degrees for the corners. You will be able to fill in tiny gaps with caulking, but you want the cuts to line up neatly, with as few gaps as possible. Apply glue to the back of the chair rail and the mouldings. This will prevent the wood from warping after it is secured to the wall. Apply the wood strips to the wall and nail them into place. Allow caulking and putty to dry, and then paint.

Main-Floor Family Room

Main-floor family rooms have become more and more popular. A living room can serve the same function, but many people like to have an additional space, usually just off the kitchen, where they can watch TV, read or just kick back. Main-floor family rooms are relaxed spaces that allow the living room to stay a bit more formal. If you have one of these main-floor family rooms, it certainly factors into the value of your home, but there isn't a lot you can do to improve its value—other than making it open to the kitchen if it isn't already and making sure it is the appropriate size. It should be roomy enough to accommodate the whole family.

Many people with older homes build an addition for a family room, which raises questions about additions and added value (see chapter 6).

Bedrooms

When it comes to bedrooms and how—and whether—they might add value to your home, you really need to think about only two things: the number of bedrooms in the house and the size of the bedrooms.

The most popular search in real estate listings is for homes with three bedrooms and two baths. Indeed, the sweet spot with bedrooms seems to be three or four. Five or more bedrooms will give you diminishing returns. In other words, your house is not going to get a whole lot more valuable if it has five or more bedrooms. But if you drop below three, it is going to be off the search list of a lot of people, meaning its competitive edge in the marketplace is weakened. I've seen a good number of older homes in which people have eliminated a small third bedroom so that they can expand the bathroom or maybe one of the other bedrooms. Unless you can put another bedroom in an attic space or elsewhere, this isn't a great idea. By removing that third bedroom, you have effectively made your home less attractive to families—which are, of course, a huge part of the house market.

Building codes vary from province to province and state to state, but many require a bedroom to be a minimum of 70 square feet (with a minimum window size and a closet). But the ideal *minimum* size of a bedroom, as far as I'm concerned, is 100 square feet. And how big is big enough? I suggest 200 square feet. Anything bigger than this will just not give much of a return on the space. But of course, the shape of the room is key as well. You want something as square as possible so that furniture can be easily arranged. Certainly, you don't want any wall to be more than 25 percent longer than the width of the room (so 10 feet by 12 works, but 8 by 15 doesn't).

In a bedroom, you do need to have a window. Its size should equal 5 percent of the floor space, and 2½ square feet of that window needs to open for ventilation. So a bedroom measuring 100 square feet needs a window that is at least 5 square feet. Anything less than this reduces the value of the space. Likewise, closet space should equal at least 10 percent of the floor space. So our 100-square-foot room would have a closet two feet deep by five feet wide. A walk-in closet is a bonus, as is an ensuite washroom.

A bedroom needs to have a source of heat—whether a rad or a vent. And this heat source should be on an arc-volt breaker. (If you are building a new bedroom and do not wire accordingly, you may be violating a building code in your region.)

There are no rules when it comes to flooring in a bedroom, but the most popular choice is some kind of solid surface, as opposed to wall-to-wall carpeting. Wall-to-wall has fallen out of favour in recent years because it can harbour dust and dust mites that aggravate allergies. Many people choose to warm up a solid-surface bedroom floor with an area rug, so hardwood or laminate (and, in some moist, warm climates, tile) adds value to the space; wall-to-wall carpeting does not.

Other features in a bedroom, like built-ins, window seats, fireplaces and ceiling fans, are nice touches, but they don't add value to your property as most people don't see these as necessities.

Laundry Room

In any home these days, a laundry area is a necessity. (In fact, even with apartments, most building codes require that a separate laundry area be included in the design of each unit.) In houses, the laundry room has worked its way up over the years—it's moved out of the basement to the main floor and has even migrated to the second floor or near the bedrooms.

It makes sense. As our lives have become more and more hectic, we want to travel less to do our chores. Convenience is so important to us that main- or top-floor laundry rooms are seen as a sign of a modern home, adding value and giving significant return on investment. In other words, we're willing to pay for convenience.

As far as adding value to your home, the master is the most important bedroom as it will generally be the buyer's room. If you are looking to add extras such as custom shelving in a walk-in closet, built-in window benches or luxury lighting fixtures, this is the bedroom to focus on!

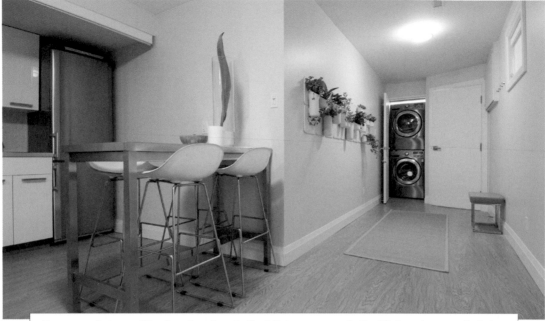

For convenience, putting laundry close to the kitchen, or even in the kitchen, is a smart choice.

Despite our acknowledgement of this once-neglected space, the basic function of the laundry room hasn't changed—it's just a place to wash, dry and fold our clothes and linens. For that reason, it's a good idea not to go over the top with this space, but rather to stick with the basics. That means a washer, dryer, a little bit of storage (perhaps cupboards over the appliances and a place to stash an ironing board) and a sink. In tight spaces, closets can be retrofitted to house a washer and dryer—putting the appliances side by side, if the closet is wide with a double door, or using stackable washers and dryers in a narrow, one-door closet. Remember that your best bet is to get the laundry out of the basement without eating up a lot of valuable main- or second-storey floor space. Putting in a more elaborate laundry room is a nice luxury, but not a good investment.

Where is the best location for a laundry room? On the main floor, anywhere off the kitchen makes sense, as does a mudroom, back vestibule or off the garage. On a second floor or in the bedroom area of a house, you should try to position a laundry so that it backs onto a bathroom and not a bedroom. You don't want the laundry close to sleeping areas because of the noise. (While you can now get super-quiet washing machines, there isn't much you can do about zippers banging around in the dryer.)

And while a main- or upper-floor laundry room can and probably should be a fairly simple space, it is not a simple renovation. The washer and dryer use a lot of power and, of course, water. Keeping the laundry room close to the kitchen or a washroom makes sense because it needs to be close to existing plumbing. It also needs good ventilation. Laundry generates significant amounts of heat and moisture, but blowing air from the dryer back into the house is a huge no-no because of all the moisture this will introduce to your home. Ventilation to the outside is a must. The ventilation hose should be a rigid metal. This is probably what is required by law in your area, and if it's not, it soon will be. A rigid metal vent decreases the buildup of lint. Lint that collects in dryer vents poses a significant fire hazard. Your laundry room should also feature a floor drain, which requires a primer line. The primer line will flow water into the C-trap of the drain, creating a seal that keeps sewer gases from backing up into your home (because this won't be a heavily used drain, a drain without a primer line will allow water from the trap to evaporate, leaving an open passage-way for gases to move up).

When planning your laundry room reno, also give some thought to the position of the washer and dryer. If they are side by side, you want to make sure that the doors open so that you can transfer clothes from the washer to the dryer without having to move around any doors. (If both units are front-loading, this means the doors should open in opposite directions, away from each other.) Some front-loading washers and dryers have doors that can be mounted on either side of the opening. Others are fixed, so check the appliances you have or that you plan to buy before you design your laundry space.

And one final word on laundry rooms: many people put laundry rooms into additions or existing sunrooms. If these spaces are not heated, a heating source must be added when the washer is installed or you may risk frozen water pipes and all the damage that can be produced by them.

Interior Hardware, Light Fixtures and Other Finishes

In the chapter on kitchens, I talked about how changing out your cabinet hardware can give you the biggest bang for your home-improvement buck. The same is actually true for all of the hardware in your house. Upgrading door handles and knobs throughout your house is an affordable way to give your interior space a fresh and modern look of luxury. In fact, I'm always amazed at how often prospective tenants comment on these finishes when they inspect a rental property. But it makes sense. We usually think about the impact a space makes in terms of what it *looks* like. But door hardware adds a second sense to the impression—the *feel* of a clean, quality knob or handle can make a strong impression. And door hardware can be a DIY project. Usually, the new set can simply be fitted into the holes left by the older set. If larger holes are required, be careful not to chisel too much wood from the hole, or the mechanism won't work properly. Just as important, always put the knobs on the doors before you close them. You'd be surprised how many people I've seen lock themselves into a room by closing the door to check a fit before putting the knob on. I usually help them get out. But not right away.

New, stylish light fixtures also go a long way towards updating the look of a home, and they don't have to cost a lot. Even new receptacles and switches can add to the clean and modern look of a home. When I am upgrading a property, I use the switches that have the large, flat, rectangular switches and receptacles that have the same rectangular centres. And I opt for white.

Small touches add up. Good quality hardware, door levers, modern light switches and dimmer switches are all simple and inexpensive ways to add value.

The home pictured in these next two spreads underwent a huge transformation—without any major construction! We simply refinished the hardwood floors, painted the walls and replaced light fixtures, curtains and curtain rods.

Chapter 5

THE FURNACE OR UTILITIES ROOM

I'd put money on it that this isn't the first chapter you turned to. Let me admit that there is nothing sexy about wiring or hot water heaters. And I'll even acknowledge that you don't often see a prospective tenant or homebuyer get pumped about a property after spotting an updated electrical panel in the basement (except maybe me). But honestly, if you read only one chapter in this book, I would suggest that it be this one. Why? Because you can't increase the value of your home by doing renos in the kitchen, bath or anywhere else if your home is losing value because its mechanics are outdated or in bad repair. Every informed home-buyer is going to demand an inspection before finalizing an offer. Finding out that the home needs a new water heater or has an inadequate water supply is going to bring everyone back to the bargaining table—and ultimately reduce the house price. But even more important, while shabby kitchen cabinets or a crumbling porch might devalue your property, faulty wiring or damaged gas lines can endanger the lives of everyone in your home. And safety should always trump any other considerations when thinking about a house. Attention to the wiring, water service and gas supply is an absolute must for property owners. And there are other utilities, like central vacuum, air conditioning, fireplaces and heat recovery systems that are not only little luxuries but may also add value to your home.

Electrical

According to the National Fire Protection Agency, one in 10 house fires in the U.S. is caused by faulty wiring or electrical distribution. And just as sobering, electrical fires are second only to incendiary or suspicious causes in the total cost of property damage that they produce. But the most frightening thing about any home fire is the danger it poses to those living in the house. No doubt about it, electrical work that is in poor condition is the number one safety hazard in the home. That's why the "return on investment" for electrical work goes far beyond financial calculations, as far as I'm concerned.

That said, if the wiring in your house is in bad shape, your property value is sinking fast. While home sellers are tempted to do quick fixes that will make their homes look as if they have been updated, savvy buyers are going to ask for a building inspection, which will inform them about the true state of the wiring. And they know that if they are faced with having to rewire a home after purchase, they will have to shell out as much as $20,000. That's why "updated electrical" is a huge selling feature for a home, and one that buyers put high value on. But how do you know if you need an electrical upgrade?

The first thing to do is check the electrical panel used to distribute power in your home. The panel will give you a clue about the age of the wiring in the house. If the panel contains fuses, the wiring is old. It may even be knob-and-tube wiring. That old system employed porcelain knobs and tubes to attach copper wire to the walls and conduct it through joists and studs. It was used in homes from about 1880 to the 1930s. There are a number of drawbacks to knob-and-tube wiring (including the fact that it doesn't feature a grounding conductor that will return any extra energy back to the panel and will direct energy from a short circuit to ground), but the primary problem is that it just wasn't designed to handle the amount of electricity the modern home uses. If you have knob and tube in your home, it *needs* to be replaced. (Most insurance companies won't provide coverage if a home still has knob-and-tube wiring).

The panel will give you a clue as to the age of the wiring, but it can't tell you the whole story. It is relatively easy to replace a panel, so even a panel with breakers might be attached to much older wiring. (Wiring is much more difficult to replace than a panel.) I always check the service and the amount of power coming into any house I'm considering purchasing. The main breaker on the panel should have a number on it. In older homes, this might say

60 amps. Sixty amps is no longer considered sufficient—most insurance companies, in fact, won't provide you with a policy unless the service is upgraded to at least 100 amps. So if your panel says 60 amps, there is no question about it—you need to upgrade your wiring. But most houses these days have 100-amp service. Large homes, or homes with pools and hot tubs, typically require 200 amps. (So if you are thinking of adding a pool or an addition to an older home, you may have to think about rewiring the house as well.)

After you've checked the panel, take a look at the wires coming out of the box. This will be a lot easier if your panel is in an unfinished basement or garage, but even in a finished space, you should be able to tell if you have a dedicated line going to each of your major appliances (which is necessary so that lines are not overtaxed). What should give you cause for concern is if you see many appliances or too many rooms running off the same breaker. If your wiring is exposed, you can see evidence of this in the number of junction boxes running off the wires. The fewer junction boxes, the better.

The next thing to check is the wire itself. The wiring is usually stamped with printing, identifying what material it is made from. In the 1960s and 1970s, aluminum wire was popular. The problem with aluminum wiring is that it expands and contracts more than copper wire, and electrical fixtures and appliances, most of which had copper connection points, were not modified to accommodate these connections. What's more, in many houses, aluminum wires are connected directly to copper wires. When these two different metals meet—either in a fixture or where the wires connect—corrosion (oxidation) of one of the metals will occur. And because the two metals have different rates of expansion, the connections can become loose. These two things can cause sparking, arcing and heat buildup—all of which are fire hazards. Fortunately, aluminum wiring can be modified to render it safe, sparing you the trouble of having to remove it. It can be pigtailed with copper wire to prevent loosening. A non-oxidizing compound can also be added to all the connections between the aluminum and copper wires so that the two metals don't corrode where they touch. Electrical fixtures can be modified as well.

Your home's wiring should also be grounded. If you have outlets that have only two-prong plugs, you can be certain there is ungrounded wiring in the house. But three-prong plugs are no guarantee that the wiring within the outlet is grounded. You can test each outlet with a circuit tester by placing the red probe in the smaller of the two straight holes and the black probe in the larger one. A light on the tester should come on to indicate that the circuit is grounded. If no light comes on, meaning your wiring is ungrounded, you need to have your wiring checked (and rewired) or your outlets changed to modified GFCI (ground fault circuit interrupter) units—the outlets with the red and black TEST and RESET buttons.

In newer homes, there is often a sticker or a label on the panel stating who did the electrical work and when it was last inspected. If this is missing, you may want to have an inspection made to make sure that everything was done properly and that the electrical work in your house is safe.

While you can check for clues about the state of your home's wiring, it is really best to have a licensed electrician carry out an inspection if you have any doubts at all. And if you do decide to do an electrical upgrade, the work should be performed and inspected by a licensed electrician as well. Keep in mind that building codes are changing all the time, and only a professional electrician can guarantee that the work being done will be up to code.

And finally, if you suspect that the wiring in your house is not up to par, I urge you to do something about it—*fast*. An electrician I met recently told me about a friend of his who had just purchased a house. This guy was an electrician too and was able to get a real bargain on the property because the wiring badly needed an upgrade. While many of the people looking at the house were turned off by that fact, he knew that he could do the work himself, to code, and save a bundle. The only problem? Just after he had taken possession, but before he moved in, the house burned to the ground. The lesson here: there's no way to tell when deficient wiring is going to fail.

Water Service

The water service in your house is not a safety issue the way wiring is, but it can sure affect your quality of life. In fact, lousy water pressure is one of the most common complaints among people with older homes. But to be accurate, it's usually not a problem of water pressure but of flow rate.

The way that water comes into your house is the way it will be distributed throughout your home. Older houses often had water supply pipes that were half an inch in diameter, but ideally your house should have at least a ¾-inch supply from the city line. This will give you enough water flow to create decent water pressure. Newer homes sometimes even have a one-inch service from the street.

The ideal scenario is to have that ¾- or one-inch line come into the house and continue straight to the water heater before it branches off to other services.

Poor water flow in an older home may be caused by things other than the line size. Over the years, corrosion of the pipes can create buildup or kinks in the line that will slow water flow. Older homes are also likely to have a line made of lead coming into the house. This isn't a flow problem, but a health concern. If you do have lead pipes, most cities have a lead pipe replacement program that will take care of taking out the lead lines and replacing them with larger lead-free pipes from the street to the edge of your property line. The homeowner is then responsible for changing the pipes from the property line into the house. These days, most of the companies that do this work use a torpedo system that tunnels underground from the street to the house so that front yards do not have to be dug up.

But does water service have any effect on the value of a home? When homebuyers come to inspect a house, they usually turn the taps on and check out the water pressure. They might consider sluggish water flow a strike against the house, but good flow typically won't get you a higher offer. And if you do have that sluggish water flow, redoing the plumbing in your home is costly, so this work doesn't usually give you a good return on investment. But this is a place where you might want to put your calculator aside—because modern, effective plumbing may not add value to the house, but it sure does add value to the quality of life you'll have in the house. And that's nothing to shrug off.

While increasing the water flow in your home by widening the line from the street and getting rid of old lead pipes will certainly benefit your whole household, there are other improvements you can make to your water service. A dedicated manifold system, which supplies each tap or appliance in your home through a dedicated line coming off your water heater and service, conserves both water and energy, but won't give you much return on investment.

Water Heater

Standard water heaters come in all different capacities—you should choose the size of your water heater based on how much water your household uses. But of course, if you are putting your house on the market, there are a few other things to consider when making your choice. A very small water heater might be of concern to a prospective homebuyer, but big is not necessarily best. Very large hot water heaters use a lot of energy—a waste if you don't actually need the capacity.

But of even more importance for cost-effective energy use is your water heater's fuel source. Electric water heaters are a huge drain on your utilities—natural gas is the much more economical way to go. And still more energy-efficient are the "hot water on demand" models. This type of system has been around a long time in Europe because of its size and reduced energy demands. It heats water as you need it rather than holding large quantities of hot water in a tank. Because on-demand systems are not storing water, they are small and can be mounted on a wall or in a closet. They will also continue to produce hot water for as long as you need it—unlike conventional hot water tanks that can be drained by high demand and will then need time to refill and heat. And because they are heating water only as you need it, they do provide energy savings.

But on-demand systems do have disadvantages. They are very expensive units to install. They can also heat up only so much water at a time, so if you have more than one appliance, shower or bath running at the same time, they may not be able to keep up with the demand for hot water. And while they do tend to use less energy, it takes 12 to 15 years' worth of energy savings to recoup the cost of the unit, so this is a long-term investment. I do, however, think that on-demand systems are the way of the future and something to consider seriously if you plan to stay in your house for the long term. They are not, however, going to get you a great ROI if you plan to sell in the near future.

There are a few things besides size and fuel type that you should check for in your hot water system. First, make sure that you have a ¾-inch line leading into the heater. You should also make sure that your hot water heater has a mixing valve on the line that comes

Energy Rebate Programs

There may be energy rebate programs available in your area that will help defray the costs of replacing appliances and fixtures such as fridges, stoves, washers, toilets and hot water heaters. Try to stay aware of what rebate offers are available—some of them can be very significant. Even if you feel that you are not in a financial position to buy a new appliance, there may be rebate programs that will give you cash to rent an energy-efficient unit.

out of the heater. This valve adds some cold water to the hot water that leaves the system, modulating the temperature so that scalding-hot water doesn't come from any of the taps in your house. These valves only cost about $75, so don't be tempted to turn down your heater's water temperature to avoid having to add the valve. You need the temperature in the tank to remain high to prevent bacteria from developing in the water. If mixing valves are not demanded by the building code in your area, they will be in the future, so making sure that you've got one now will both ensure your household's safety and save you any setbacks with the house inspection if you decide to sell.

The Furnace

If your furnace is more than 20 years old, it's time to consider replacing it. Not only will this help you avoid the nasty surprise of a furnace that gives up during a sub-zero winter night (or worse, malfunctions, allowing carbon monoxide to seep through your house), it will also save you heating costs, as new models are much more energy-efficient than furnaces of the past. And you will recoup 50 to 80 percent of the cost, according to the Appraisal Institute of Canada, if you can feature a new furnace in your listing when you sell your home.

Choosing a new furnace is not something you can usually do yourself. Typically, an HVAC expert will visit your home to determine the size and efficiency of the unit needed for your home. He or she will make sure to recommend a unit that is not overworked or underworked—in other words, that it is the most efficient furnace for the size and layout of your home.

If you are interested in energy-saving technologies, like geothermal heating systems or solar panels, keep in mind that these generally take 10 to 12 years to recoup their costs through energy savings. You may well decide that this is an investment you want to make, but these systems will not give you much return on investment when you resell your home, especially as not all homebuyers like the look of solar panels. Solar panels are less conspicuous, however, on a home in an isolated or rural area with a big roof. They work especially well when the house is facing south or southwest.

Most newly constructed houses will feature a heat recovery ventilator, which uses the stale interior air of a home to heat the fresh exterior air before it is brought into the house. In this way, it improves the air quality in homes that would otherwise be airtight and recovers much of the energy used to heat the air. But while adding a heat recovery ventilator to an older home may give you energy savings, it won't have an impact on your resale value.

Smoke and Carbon Monoxide Detectors

Like your electrical systems, smoke and carbon monoxide detectors are not things that will immediately and obviously raise your home's value, but they are essential to safeguarding your family's health and safety and are not to be overlooked.

The best systems are interconnected. That way, if an alarm goes off in the basement, it will immediately go off on the second floor as well, making sure it is heard by everyone in the house. While there are interconnected, wired-in systems that combine smoke and carbon monoxide detectors, there are also interconnected *wireless* smoke alarms on the market. But if you opt to add the wireless system, you will have to add independent carbon monoxide units.

Which leads me to make a plea: don't overlook carbon monoxide detectors. While most people do have smoke alarms, many neglect to install carbon monoxide detectors, yet they cost less than $100 and have been proven to save lives—an investment well worth making!

If you have battery-operated smoke and carbon monoxide alarms, check the batteries at least twice a year. A good rule is to change them at the same time as you change your clocks in the spring and fall.

The Best Way to Invest in Your Home: Maintenance

It's not as exciting as a spa bathroom or a walk-in wine cellar, but consistent, thorough maintenance is far and away the best way to hold and increase the value of your home. Make sure that your household budget provides for the cost of things like roof repairs, replumbing and so on. And before you embark on home renos, consider whether you need to do some basic maintenance first. There is no point in refinishing a basement if the space has moisture issues. Waterproofing the below-grade space before you do anything else will make your future finished basement much more comfortable and save you the agony of ripping out a recently installed family room because of growing mould and mildew. Likewise, a new chef's kitchen will seem a lot less appealing if the bathroom above it is leaving ugly water stains on the ceiling above the breakfast nook.

And remember that maintaining the envelope of your home—including caulking, sealing or replacing windows and doors, repairing crumbling brickwork and adding insulation in walls and roofs—will save you money over the years that can be put towards all the little extras you might want to add to your home.

Air Conditioning

Most of the return on investment figures associated with installing air conditioning in a home are pretty low. That's probably because in places like the American South, air conditioning is considered somewhat of a necessity, but in most parts of Canada it's still considered something of a luxury. But if you do it right, I believe you can get back at least 75—and as much as 100—percent of the money you spend on AC on resale. You aren't, however, going to make money by adding air conditioning to your home.

If you have forced-air heating, you can add in-duct air conditioning, but it isn't cheap. And there aren't really any ways to save money on installation—it has to be done properly. You can, however, get a greater return and avoid devaluing your property by making sure you put the outside AC fan in an area where it won't be highly visible or block laneways or other access areas. Try to have it placed at the side of your house so that it doesn't become a prominent—and unsightly—feature of your front yard. And make sure that you have a programmable thermostat so that you can use the AC efficiently and save energy.

If you have radiant heat, you can go for ductless or a window mount. Given that even installing even two of these units can be less expensive than a forced-air system, you can get your money back on resale with ductless units. Placement of these units is the key to maximizing your return with ductless air conditioning. Choose a location high in the house, where cool air can fall freely and cool the areas beneath it as well as around it. You may, for example, need only one unit, positioned near the upstairs bedrooms. The rotating fan in the unit can be positioned to circulate the air around the second floor and down the staircase.

Window-mount units, while keeping you cool, are not going to get you any return on investment.

Central Vac

A central vacuum system is a luxury, so if you are adding one to an existing home, you'll have to be really lucky to recapture your investment. The amount of labour it takes to install a central vac will simply eat up any increase in the value of the house. If, however, you are planning your home from the building stage, and you have an unfinished basement to work with, it might be worth the investment.

Sump Pump

Installing a sump-pump pit might be a great idea if you have a lot of moisture or water under the house, particularly if you want to use the basement for additional living space.

A sump-pump pit is a big hole with a weeping tile system, a barrel, a water level and a pump. When the barrel fills to a certain level, the pump turns on and pumps the water far away from the home.

Since water will collect at a building's foundation and will make its way into the basement eventually, a sump-pump pit is just part of finishing a basement in an area that has a high water table. It doesn't necessarily return the money invested in it, but it protects the value of your entire home.

Changing a Furnace Air Filter

While this is a super-easy bit of home maintenance, it's often overlooked. Regular changing of your furnace filter, however, can really help improve the air quality of your home. You should change your filter every three to five months. If you have pets, a lot of traffic in and out of your home, or are particularly sensitive to dust and pollen, change your filter more frequently. Generally, you also want to change your filter more frequently in the winter, when the furnace is running all of the time. If you have your AC running regularly in the summer, you will need to change the filter more often then as well.

When purchasing a new filter, make sure you get the right size by comparing it to the old filter. Air filters vary in quality and range in price from $2 to $50. Very inexpensive filters are thin and don't provide a great deal of filtration for fine particulate or pollen. They will, however, filter out hair, pet hair and larger particles of dust. They will also provide more airflow than the denser, more expensive varieties.

Higher-priced filters work well on pollen and fine dust, but they also restrict airflow. I usually opt for a mid-priced filter to get the best of both worlds.

To change the filter, first turn off the furnace at the thermostat. If the furnace is running, there will be pressure on the filter, making it more difficult to pull out. The filter may also bend with the pressure, sending dust into your furnace as you pull it out. After turning off the furnace, look to the bottom of the unit, where the air returns enter. There will be a one-inch slot there, which may have a small metal cap over it. Remove the cap if so and carefully pull the old filter from the slot.

Before sliding the new filter into the slot, check to make sure you've got it turned in the right direction. They are built to have the airflow going in one direction, which is marked with an arrow. The arrow should be pointing towards the furnace.

Put the dirty filter directly into a plastic bag without bending or crushing it and take it outside to the garbage.

Chapter 6

ADDITIONS AND CREATING EXTRA LIVING SPACE

Are additions a good way to add value to your home? Frankly, in most cases, no. Many appraisers suggest that an expansion can recover 50 to 75 percent of its cost, and this is the range I see as well. Given that I have a good track record beating the Appraisal Institute's estimates, this may surprise you. But there are good reasons for the difficulty in recouping what you spend on an expansion. The first is that most people use additions to add features to their homes that other buyers don't necessarily want to pay more for—things like sunrooms, offices or spa-sized bathrooms (the main-floor family room is more likely to get you to the high end of the AIC's range of return on investment).

And second, unless your lot is huge, additions eat up backyards and garden areas, which are still very important to homebuyers. Most people still want outdoor space, especially people with children. Of course, this depends somewhat on where you live. In the suburbs, people expect a relatively large backyard, so when selling a house, it's a necessity. In dense urban areas, outdoor space is often seen as a bonus. And in every municipality, there will be bylaws that outline the required ratios of outdoor and indoor space.

All that being said, if your addition will take up most of your backyard, you might want to rethink your plans. Perhaps moving to a larger house on a larger lot makes more sense. In other words, the added value you might achieve with an addition may very well be eliminated by the reduction in your property's value because it now has so little yard.

But there are exceptions. While you don't want your house to be the biggest in the neighbourhood (most people who want large homes are likely looking in areas with other large homes), if your lot is really big, then using a bit of it for a house expansion may add value. Just remember that real estate prices tend to even out across a neighbourhood—larger homes see their values reduced or flattened, while the resale prices of smaller homes tend to get drawn up to the median.

Also, if your home is 1,000 square feet or less, or in an urban area where homes are relatively small, ample backyard space is not expected and indoor space is at a premium, it may make sense to put on an addition. Just make sure that the added space provides features that buyers look for—a third or fourth bedroom (maybe a master bedroom with an ensuite bath and ample closet space), a second bathroom, a main- or top-floor laundry room or a family room leading off the kitchen.

There are other ways to add living space to a home, and many can be achieved without expanding your home's footprint. Here are my five favourite living space extensions, ranked from highest to lowest potential return on investment:

1. Converting an attic to a bedroom/bathroom combo. This reno doesn't require you to remove walls or ceilings or lose outdoor space.
2. Creating a basement apartment (see Income Suites in chapter 8). As with an attic conversion, you won't lose outdoor space or have to remove interior or exterior walls.
3. Building an addition to accommodate a larger kitchen, with an extra room or bathroom above it.
4. Adding another storey—a top-up—so that a bungalow becomes a two-storey home, or a two-storey home becomes a three-storey one. (This kind of addition typically doubles the size of the home without changing its footprint. It works well in older neighbourhoods with small or moderately sized lots and existing two- or three-storey homes. It is, however, a costly reno.)
5. Finishing the basement for extra living space (rec rooms, additional bedroom, etc.).

In order to finish a basement or an attic, however, you really need the height of the ceiling to be no less than seven feet over 75 percent of the space.

Finishing a basement has been a popular way to add living space to homes for many years, so it's worth discussing it a little further in relation to increasing your home's value. While finishing a basement can be less expensive than building an addition, it can still be tough to recoup 100 percent of your expenditures. (The AIC says the average return on investment is between 50 and 75 percent.) To recapture as much of your investment as you can, make sure that when you are finishing your basement, you are addressing the limited elements of your home. If you have only one washroom, add another on the lower level. If you have only two bedrooms, build one down there. (The most desired listing is "three bedrooms, two bathrooms." A basement renovation that allows your house to match that description might not get you a lot more money on resale but might generate more interest in your listing.) If your storage on the main or second floor is limited, add storage space to your finished basement. If your kitchen is cramped, a second kitchen might be in order.

To transform a basement space into a living space, you need adequate ceiling height. You can drop down to as low as 6 feet 5 inches under support beams, but remember when measuring for this that the height has to take into account the ceiling drywall and flooring that will be installed.

Turning an attic into a bedroom is a great way to add value to your home. Attics with dormer windows, which provide more space, generally lend themselves well to this kind of conversion. Carpeting in an attic room not only warms the space but also provides sound absorption for the rooms below.

Other popular finished-basement features are a play area for the kids, and office space. Keep in mind, however, that these are all bonuses that can make your home more attractive but typically are not going to outperform the cost of adding them.

Is there anything to avoid when finishing a basement? Absolutely. Avoid wood panelling, for one. And wet bars are just a novelty. Their very limited use usually translates into limited appeal to buyers. Drop ceilings are fine, although they never look as clean as drywall. They do, however, make it easier to get to the mechanics in the basement. Just make sure you replace stained or damaged panels. And while many people like to finish their basements with wall-to-wall carpeting, I'm not a huge fan of that choice. You need a really dry basement for carpeting, as it will hold any moisture that is absorbed into it. Even if your basement is dry, you need to have the right underpad for carpeting—one that has a lining that keeps moisture from the concrete away from the carpet. (For more ideas about basement flooring, check page 163 in chapter 8.)

And finally, if you have a low ceiling in your basement (under seven feet), a finished basement just may not be an economical renovation. Digging out a basement generally costs about $300 per linear foot. Only certain homes in high-priced areas are going to recapture that kind of cost. Digging out your basement may well be worth it to you, but you need to accept that this renovation will not pay for itself on resale.

A basement renovation in process. After insulation and vapour barrier, the drywall can go up.

Additions and Adding Extra Living Space DIYs

Almost by definition, putting on additions and finishing attics and basements are big jobs that usually require structural changes, wiring and drywalling. While structural work and wiring require trade licences, even drywalling, taping and mudding demand the skills of a professional. For these reasons, additions usually provide DIY jobs only for the very skilled do-it-yourselfers. Of course, there may be opportunities to do any of the other DIY projects mentioned throughout this book in those spaces. And large-scale renovations like this provide the chance to do one of the most fun parts of any reno: the demolition.

You can tear down old drywall, pull up carpet or flooring, take out windows or doors, and fill Dumpsters with this and other garbage. Just be careful not to touch wiring or plumbing. And don't handle asbestos or any material that shows significant amounts of mould. Materials coated with lead paint can also be hazardous to take apart. You will usually only find lead paint in the interiors of older homes (pre-1960). To be on the safe side, you should wear a mask during demolition. Also make sure that you are wearing a hard hat, gloves, steel-toed boots and eye protection. Remember, you don't know how things have been built or what surprises might be hidden behind walls and ceilings, so use extreme caution when demolishing anything.

Chapter 7

HOUSE EXTERIORS

As a landlord and a real estate investor, I look at hundreds of houses every year. I am now pretty savvy about assessing properties, and I know that you can't always judge a book by its cover. But when I first started searching for income properties, I would pull up in front of a house, take one look at the exterior and decide right then and there whether it was worth going in. If the paint was peeling, the front porch crumbling or the roof in obvious need of repair, I'd just keep going. A lot of buyers never get past that reaction, which means that for anyone selling a house, it's not always what's inside that counts!

People assume (often rightly) that the outside of a property is a good indication of what is inside. If the exterior shows some pride of ownership, then the inside is going to show the same care and attractiveness too. The front is obviously the most essential part of the house as far as "curb appeal" goes—that means everything from the grass to the windows to the roof. But the lesson we should take from people's reaction to the front is that the exterior of a home—all of it—really does matter to homebuyers. In fact, *Remodeling* magazine's annual Cost vs. Value Reports consistently list siding and window and door replacements as giving the best returns on investment of any home improvement projects. That certainly suggests that you should be thinking about the outside of your home as well as the interior when you are looking to add value, and I would argue that by doing the right sorts of things on the exterior of your home, you can consistently hit those top Appraisal Institute of Canada numbers and avoid making expensive mistakes. In truth, not every renovation can turn you a profit, but you should always get as great an ROI as you can.

Roofs

It may be a little hard to get excited about the idea of "investing" in a new roof, but your roof shouldn't be ignored either. The condition of a roof is, of course, a maintenance issue. A roof in poor repair can cause leaking, which in turn can lead to damaged ceilings and walls, mould, rot and all of those pests that love damp wood (such as termites and carpenter ants). Allowing a roof to stay in a state of disrepair is to allow your home to depreciate in value.

You can assess the state of your roof by inspecting the shingles. Most North American homes have asphalt shingles, which are supposed to have a lifespan of about 20 to 25 years. In reality, however, high sun and wind exposure can reduce this life expectancy—any roof at least 15 years old may well be showing its age. Roofs with curling, lifting or missing shingles need attention as soon as possible. Ditto if there are moss and other flora sprouting up there.

But keep in mind that while a roof in good condition protects your housing investment, an attractive, stylish roof can also contribute a decent return on investment (at least the high end of the AIC's 50-to-80 percent range).

When putting on a new roof, you need to consider the type of shingle material, the style of shingle and the colour. The colour needs to be in keeping with the style of your home and the rest of the exterior colours. While a bright red roof looks great on a barn or on a waterfront cottage, it will no doubt devalue your suburban backsplit (although it might give the neighbours something to talk about for a while).

Asphalt shingles are available in two styles: standard, which are completely uniform in size and shape, and "designer." Designer shingles have varied or uneven sizing that gives the roof a more textured, dimensional look. Some brands feature variegated colours for added visual interest. There are also designer shingles that resemble slate or wooden-shake roofs. I usually opt for the designer shingles. I find they have a cleaner, sleeker look but don't cost significantly more, so they are worth it to generate some extra resale value.

There are roofing options other than asphalt shingles, of course. Slate, cedar, steel, copper and red clay are all more expensive than asphalt, but they have their advantages.

Metal roofs—particularly copper and steel—last a very long time. In fact, most will outlive their owners, and some argue that if you are planning to stay in the house forever, they are worth the money. But the problem is that if you do decide to sell, most people won't pay any extra for a metal roof, so your investment won't pay off. Copper, however, may be worth the added cost if you use it as a design feature in small areas that are highly visible. While it turns green after 20 years or so, this patina can be as appealing as, or more attractive than, the original copper colour.

Like metal, slate can lend an air of quality and elegance to a home. But while slate roofs may last anywhere from 50 to 200 years, they are very expensive to install and cost a fortune to repair. For that reason, an older slate roof is likely to pull a house's value down—no one likes the prospective of shelling out big bucks to fix it. Because of the very high initial and maintenance costs, slate roofs are very rare these days, and they are not going to yield any return on investment if you splurge for a new one.

Cedar shakes and shingles can last from 15 to 50 years. They perform well in windy areas and add more insulation value to the roof than metal roofs or asphalt shingles do. But cedar is considerably more expensive than asphalt shingles, so most people use cedar as an accent— over a porch or gable or around a turret, for example. (Some people opt for copper accents in the same way.) Cedar can give a home a distinctive look, but there is usually not a lot of bang for the buck associated with this kind of embellishment.

Cedar shakes and shingles can provide attractive accents to roofs, but remember that to maintain value, you must scrape and repaint if the paint or stain cracks or peels.

Clay tiles are more expensive than asphalt, but compared to steel or slate, the additional cost is reasonable. In really windy areas (coastal Florida, for example), clay will perform better than asphalt shingles (which have a tendency to become airborne in extreme weather). In areas with more moderate wind patterns, clay roofs are usually a style choice and, for that reason, are not likely to get you much of a return on your investment.

The best way to decide on the roofing material you want is to determine what kinds of roofs are most common in your area. Going with the most popular option will not only get you the greatest return on your investment; it will also ensure that there are plenty of local professional roofers with the knowledge and equipment necessary to maintain and repair your roofing material.

A final word about roofs: they really aren't DIY projects. Not only is roofing hot, dirty work, but considerable expertise is needed to do a good job that is up to code. While completely replacing shingles is usually best, in some places, new asphalt shingles can be layered on top of old ones—but only a certain number of times. A professional roofer will be able to assess the weight limit and fire hazard of layering, if that is a route you want to explore. And employing a professional roofer with plenty of experience in the area is essential when you are replacing or repairing a flat roof.

GUTTERS AND SOFFIT & FASCIA

As far as curb appeal goes, the only things that matter with eavestroughs or rain gutters and soffit and fascia are that they are clean, intact and in some colour that complements the roof and exterior of the house. And in order to avoid devaluing the house, they have to be in good working order. Nothing whispers "neglect" more loudly than rain gutters choked with leaves or morphing into little gardens, seedlings and weeds sprouting out of the clogged debris.

Eavestroughs need to be tight to the house, with the drip edge under the roof's shingles running into them. If drainage from the roof is allowed to flow behind the eavestrough, rot can develop. The gutters should also slope towards the downspout, which should drain the water at least five feet away from the house. If the downspouts and eavestrough allow water to flow closer than that, you can get foundation issues, rot and termites.

Soffit and fascia must be free from gaps and holes (which can be great invitations to birds, squirrels and other critters) and vent properly to the attic space.

Siding

Brick, stucco, stone, vinyl, aluminum, plastic or wood siding—they all have their advantages. And a lot of homes have been built with a mix of these materials.

Sidings are the least expensive and are at the bottom of the range as far as quality and desirability go. But they are fairly easy to repair, and you can paint them (even vinyl) to freshen up your home's exterior look. Depending on the real estate values in your area, they may be a reasonable choice, but they don't generally add any value to your home.

Stucco is generally more expensive than siding, but it is a versatile product that can go over old brick, so it's often chosen as a way to repair or update an older exterior. It also has some insulation value (especially the new forms that use a Styrofoam base). It shows up in newly built homes as well, sometimes combined with brick or stone areas of the exteriors. Stucco can also be dressed up with crown mouldings and other sorts of window trims and details. And like siding, stucco can be painted as the years go on, allowing you to update the exterior of your house. But applying a stucco exterior is trickier than it looks. If it's not done right, it will bubble and peel, and these kinds of defects usually need a professional to fix. So my advice is that you *start* with the professional and not try to do this yourself! And if at all possible, try to keep the original brick. Brick is always in style.

STONE AND BRICK

Natural stone is at the highest end of the cost and quality range. And there's no doubt about it—in a high-end neighbourhood, a well-chosen stone can give a house an air of luxury and quality. But a lot of people look for a brick house, as brick is tested and true. Like stone, brick has some insulation value, lasts a very long time and is relatively maintenance free (unless it's painted—more about painting brick in a moment). Brick homes tend to keep their value. So building a new home with a brick exterior, or adding or repairing one on an existing home, will give you plenty of return on investment.

That being said, brick adds value to your home if it's in good repair, so you need to check on its condition from time to time. Pay particular attention to the mortar. Mortar is used to keep the bricks apart, and it has to be weaker than the brick to allow for brick movement and so that it doesn't damage the brick itself. But because it is weaker, it deteriorates faster

Refreshing a tired exterior is a great way to both add curb appeal and advertise the quality of your home's interior. The details matter: pay attention to the porch, walkway, gardens, house number, mailbox, etc., as well as the condition of the bricks and siding.

than the brick. The good news is that mortar is easily fixed: "repointing" can replace missing or cracked mortar. And the cost of repointing pays big dividends—it preserves an asset and therefore adds great value.

Chimneys are usually the first places to show signs of damage to brick. Looking at your chimney will give you a good sense of the condition of the rest of your bricks and mortar. If there are holes and inconsistency in the mortar, or if it is set back more than half an inch from the brick, it's time to get work done. But make sure that you hire professional masons—there are a lot of inexperienced people out there willing to do repointing, but if they use mortar that is too hard, the bricks will end up crumbling. And do make sure that you have a look at your mortar colour options. You will want to match the existing mortar (a custom colour may need to be mixed) and keep with the period look of your home. Bright white mortar in between old, weathered bricks looks jarring and unnatural. And this is not a DIY project. Repointing is an art. You don't want your fledgling technique to put its own unique stamp on the front of your home!

If the bricks themselves are damaged, they can be replaced. Swapping out a few bricks isn't hard, but replacing a lot of them can be a time-consuming and costly effort. Because of this, a lot of people opt to paint over the bricks instead. But I usually caution against this. The value of having a brick house is decreased if the brick is painted. And while prospective buyers who want a brick exterior can consider sandblasting off the paint, that's a big job that adds to the expense of repairing the brick and will certainly factor into the price they are willing to pay for the house.

If your brick still has structural integrity, I suggest that you invest in repairing it. Brick will never go out of style, and the money spent on saving the brick protects your house's worth. If the brick no longer has structural integrity, then you have a bigger decision to tackle. Rebricking a home is so expensive that, for the most part, it's usually not worth it. As they say, it's hard to raise a sunken ship. If the brick is shot, you will probably have to start looking for affordable alternatives, like stucco (as discussed above). If you are embarking on a new build, you might also consider engineered stone. Its perceived value by homebuyers is as high as that of natural stone, and the price points are pretty similar for quality products. But stay away from the very inexpensive versions of engineered stone. These tend to look bad in no time flat, and they are going to cost you more in labour and repair work than the better stone products available.

Brick exteriors are always an asset if they are in good condition. Repointing damaged brick and mortar is a great way to retain value in your home, but it is typically not a DIY project.

When deciding how to repair or refresh your home's exterior, you can use the same rule of thumb as I suggested for roofs: check out what kinds of exteriors most houses in your neighbourhood have. If they are all brick, then stucco or siding may diminish your house value. If most of the houses surrounding yours have stucco or siding, you will be safe with these options, but a stone or brick exterior in good condition may set your house apart and increase its value.

Windows

Windows can contribute a huge amount to your home's curb appeal, and they are an extremely important part of a house's functional exterior. Because of their aesthetic and practical function, windows are something that buyers always pay attention to, and so homeowners concerned with maintaining and increasing their home value should be looking at them as well. While the Appraisal Institute of Canada numbers suggest that your ROI for windows will be in the range of 50 to 75 percent, new quality windows can certainly add value to a property—in other words, get you over 100 percent in ROI.

In fact, the only type of older windows that retain their value are stained- or leaded-glass ones. But even these are less popular the farther north you go, as energy efficiency in colder areas tends to trump all other considerations.

Energy efficiency is something everyone expects in windows these days. The new energy-rated windows are filled with argon gas and the panes are treated with a coating to protect against ultraviolet rays. These windows provide insulation, keeping warm air in during the cold months and the sun's heating rays out during the hot months, lowering your energy bills in the process.

Aside from their energy-conserving value, new windows also offer a staggering variety of styles and designs. The style of your house will usually dictate the kind of window you choose. But the different styles also all function differently and serve different purposes. Casement windows allow the glass panes to swing out like doors, providing some of the best ventilation for their size. The awning version of the casement window swings out like a tent, preventing rain from hitting the screen or entering the house. Sliding windows can open left and right or up and down. Some also have features that allow the panes to tilt out for

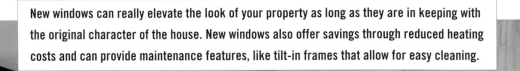

New windows can really elevate the look of your property as long as they are in keeping with the original character of the house. New windows also offer savings through reduced heating costs and can provide maintenance features, like tilt-in frames that allow for easy cleaning.

easy cleaning. Sliding windows usually also allow you to pop open all of the panes for good ventilation or to transport things in and out of the house if the items are too big for your doorways. There are also fixed-pane windows that do not open and are used for increasing light. The only advantage to these windows is that they have a tight seal. And some may come with a small slider at the bottom for a little ventilation.

Of course, there are other design elements that can be added to windows, such as different framing profiles, jamb extensions, transoms and mullions. Mullions (the strips of wood or metal that divide the glass into panes) can add a lot of character to windows and give your exterior a higher-end feel. But again, pay attention to quality. Very inexpensive plastic mullions in windows can yellow and break. And because they are wedged between two sealed panes of glass, if they shift or fall out of place, you can't repair or replace them.

But an important part of making sure that your new windows really do add value to your home is proper installation. There are two methods for installing new windows. The less expensive one is to pull out the old glass but leave the frames intact. The window installer then builds a new window that fills that mould. I don't recommend this method because what you'll save on installation costs is insignificant compared to the drawbacks. First, the improved insulation value of the new windows is going to be cancelled out by the heat loss around the window. The old frames will not have the new insulation technology, and steady heat loss with occur through the frames and possibly around the seals between the old frame and the new window. And second, your new windowpanes will have their own frames, so you will have a frame within a frame, giving you much smaller windows.

The other way to install new windows is to remove the old windows and the frames— what is often referred to as "brick to brick" installation. It costs a little more, but you get the advantages of bigger windows, insulated frames and proper seals.

You can also consider enlarging the window openings themselves if you want to replace old windows with bigger ones, but this does require a building permit and specialized work that can be pricey. But the expense may be worth it if the new windows increase the light in a space and improve the exterior look of the house.

If you are looking to create more light in your home without going to the hassle and expense of expanding window openings, I have a quick trick: put windows in your exterior doors. This is absolutely the most cost-effective way to increase light and make your space feel brighter. You don't need a permit to add this kind of window, and you can even get door windows that open for ventilation. And there are plenty of new glass-panelled door styles to choose from, so this can also be an attractive accent to your home's exterior.

Front Entranceway and Porches

Everything at the front of your house should lead up to or highlight your front entrance. The front steps should be safe and appealing, with handrails on either side. The steps can be wood, concrete, composite or interlock block, but a good rule to follow is to make sure they tie in with some other element of the front area of the house. So if you have a wooden porch, go with wooden stairs. An interlocking-stone driveway or footpath can lead into interlock steps. Poured concrete steps are sturdy and relatively inexpensive, but if you are hoping to up the value of your property, they are probably not the best choice, as they tend to look a little underwhelming or "no frills." As far as the railings on a porch go, I don't typically opt for wood. It looks good in the short term, but its lifespan is quite short. Instead, I generally use plastic or aluminum railing products.

DOORS

Replacing your front door may seem like a small thing, but it can pay big dividends. In fact, *Remodeling* magazine's Cost vs. Value Reports routinely cite a new steel front door as the number one source of remodelling return on investment, with fibreglass doors not far down the list.

Front doors have a lot of impact on a home for a number of reasons. As far as curb appeal goes, everyone sees the front door. It's really the focal point for a house's facade. And of course, a well-manufactured front door with good hardware provides security for the home. Finally, many new front doors, particularly steel and fibreglass doors with tight seals, provide insulation and draft protection.

As mentioned above, many new door styles are available with generous double-paned window panels that provide an extra light source for your home. You should make sure that any exterior door in your home has a secure keyed lock with a deadbolt. Door hardware is not a place to cut corners—you need a strong, quality product, which should run you somewhere starting around $50. All exterior doors should open in—if a door swings outside, an intruder can pop the hinges to remove the door.

Steel doors give you the best ROI, largely because of their low price point (you can get a good steel door for as little as $350). Like fibreglass doors, they can be painted, giving you a certain amount of versatility. But my favourite type of front door is still solid wood. I think they look great, and man-made materials can never adequately capture the rich wood grain. And if you have an entryway that is large enough, you can add glass panels on either side of a solid wood door to allow additional light into the space. That being said, you need to pick a door with a price point that is appropriate to the total value of your house—for example, keeping door costs to about 1 or one-half of one percent of the total value of your home is a good guideline. But even in the most luxurious home, I wouldn't spend more than $2,500 on a front door.

Installing a new front door. You don't need to buy the most expensive door, but don't skip quality door hardware and locks.

FRONT PORCH

If you are lucky enough to have a front porch on your home, take advantage of this feature. Just like a back deck, adding an outdoor seating arrangement, a small table and an outdoor rug instantly provides extra living space and adds to the square footage of your home. You can even add drapes or screens to the porch to create privacy. And if selling your house, don't overlook sprucing up this part of your home. As I discussed at the beginning of the chapter, curb appeal really does have an effect on buyers, and an inviting front porch can make a great first impression.

MAILBOXES, DOORBELLS, HOUSE NUMBERS, ETC.

Mailboxes, doorbells and house numbers are all low-cost items that are well worth replacing if they are old, outdated or just unattractive. Since none of these things are going to cost you much, I suggest splurging a little to get good-quality, stylish pieces that reflect the era and style of your home. You can also paint your mailbox to renew it if it's in good repair otherwise.

Keep in mind that the elements can quickly render exterior surfaces dull and dirty. Don't overlook the impact that a fresh coat of paint can have on shutters, railings and porch floors. Just make sure that you prep the area properly and use the right exterior paint products. Your local paint store can guide you in the right direction.

And don't forget that the little extras can give you a lot of bang for your buck: a new doormat, a potted plant or window boxes are great, inexpensive ways to make your front entranceway look warm and inviting.

LIGHTING

I'm a fan of exterior lighting. It's a great way to highlight the external features of your home. And decent lighting makes it safer to enter and exit your property as well. Ideally, you will have a good light near your entry door and lighting in front of your garage. Motion-sensor lights at the side door or on the way to the backyard or back door are often a good addition. I also like uplighting on the house itself and pot lights on the porch. But frankly, these last two are bonus items that don't really add a ton of value to your home, and they are only worth the splurge if the exterior of the house is attractive enough to be worth highlighting! Really fancy external lighting like post lights and porch chandeliers are for your enjoyment only—there's not any return on investment to be had here.

And a final word about lights: Christmas lights are nice in December. I repeat, *in December*. Don't be that guy with the sad, dusty string of holiday lights hanging off the eavestrough in July.

Parking and Garages

Whether or not adding a garage will increase the value of your home depends on where you live. Garages are expected in suburban areas; in most cases, if you don't have a garage (say, in a large city), it's because you don't have the space. But if you do have room for a garage, you can expect a 50 to 75 percent return on investment, according to the Appraisal Institute of Canada, if you add one. If your home doesn't have any covered parking and you are thinking of adding something, keep in mind that in the more northerly areas of North America, garages add much more value to a home than a carport. They provide the most protection for your vehicles, but they also represent additional space for your home—for storage, work areas and so on. (You may, therefore, get a greater ROI for a garage addition if you don't have a basement.)

Much like replacing front doors, new garage doors often provide a significant return on investment, according to many estimates. Just make sure they complement the style of your house and your front door. But don't worry about the bells and whistles if your chief concern is added value—garage door openers are not going to raise your house price.

If you live in an urban area, having parking on your property may not be a given. If you don't have parking, adding off-street parking—even if it is just pad parking at the front of your house—will add to your house value. In fact, in some urban areas, parking could add $40,000 to $50,000 to a house's price tag. If you do have parking, don't get rid of it—even if you don't own a car!

Front Yards

LANDSCAPING

There are a lot of ways to go with a front yard, and what you do really depends on personal choice. But keep in mind that most homebuyers are attracted to properties that have lush green spaces around them. That's why neighbourhoods with mature trees often command higher prices.

A grass-only yard can look barren and a bit drab. Foundation plantings (low shrubs and bushes) break up the hard lines at the bases of the exterior walls and make the house appear to be integrated with the rest of the yard. But it's important that these bushes aren't touching the walls, as the house needs to breathe. Without adequate space between plants and the house, moisture can build up, inviting termites, ants and mould.

If you decide to plant a new tree, it too should be planted far enough away from the house that its mature roots won't interfere with the foundation or the plumbing. To figure out how far the roots will extend, find out how wide the canopy of the tree can become when it is mature. The roots will continue out at least as far as the longest branches. And remember that, if you already have a mature tree on your property, you should have the plumbing lines on your property scoped periodically to make sure the root system isn't causing damage to your underground pipes. That's one thing any savvy prospective buyer will insist on doing before finalizing an offer.

Some homeowners, in particular those with small front yards, may opt to get rid of grass altogether and fill this space with a variety of perennials. While these small front gardens still require some maintenance, with the right plant choices they can be less work than a lawn. But whatever you add to your front yard should include some perennials. Landscaping with only annuals means that you have to replant each year, water continually and be faced with bare dirt flower beds when everything dies in the fall. Annuals in hanging baskets and planters, however, are a simple, relatively inexpensive way to spruce up the look of a house.

If you want to add some trees, plants and shrubs to your front lawn or turn your whole front yard into a garden but are unsure of what to buy and where to place it, checking in with a garden centre or nursery is always a good idea. If you provide your property measurements and elevations, many of these businesses will suggest a list of plants for you and may even draw up a landscaping plan for a fee, which is then deducted from the cost of your purchases.

Tip: If an attractive, low-maintenance garden appeals to you, choose perennials that are native to your area and that are drought-tolerant. And surround your plantings (whatever they are) with landscape fabric covered with a layer of shredded bark mulch. This combination will keep weeds down and moisture in.

HARDSCAPING

Hardscaping refers to all of the outdoor features of your property that are man-made, rather than landscaping or plant life or natural features. Hardscaping in your front yard might include the driveway, walkways, retaining walls, pillars and steps.

There are essentially four types of driveways that you can have. From least expensive to most costly, they are: dirt or gravel, asphalt, concrete (20 to 50 percent ROI, according to the Appraisers Institute of Canada) and interlock (25 to 50 percent). But with each higher price point comes an increase in quality and the look of luxury the driveway lends the property. The value of your home and of the properties in your area should dictate how much money you spend on its exterior.

That being said, I like to use interlock whenever possible on the properties I'm upgrading. Permacon makes some of the best interlocking stone on the market—well constructed and versatile, it comes in a great selection of styles, with innovative new products showing up all the time. I usually choose this engineered stone over flagstone and slate simply because it performs better than natural stone. While interlock and natural stone both need good bases (more on this below), natural stone, even with a decent base, is more likely than interlock to heave, shift, crack or settle into ruts where the car tires rest. (Remember, you'll get more of your money back on this hardscaping if it looks recently done.) Slate and flagstone also tend to chip, resulting in wasted material during the installation. And because of the stones' irregular shapes, they are time-consuming to lay.

If you opt for interlock, just make sure that you pick a classic, timeless look. The brick and keystone shapes were very popular for a while, but now they tend to look dated. Likewise, certain colours of interlock seem a little tired. To avoid this, I try to choose products that look as much like natural stone as possible. (Natural stone never really goes out of fashion.) And I always pick something that complements the exterior of the house. Keep in mind that you can add visual interest with some of the plainer shapes by mixing and matching them, by laying them in patterns like herringbone or by creating inlaid patterns in spots.

It is possible to lay small areas (like footpaths) of interlock yourself, but driveways require insulation, a 12-inch, tightly packed base and appropriate drainage. (Walkways need only a six-inch base.) Unless you have the experience and the right equipment, this is not really a DIY project. The same goes for retaining walls and pillars, which need careful construction and tamping to make them secure.

Interlock driveway, walkways and landscaping totally transformed the front of this house. I like to add three-dimensional elements like small walls and planters for greater effect.

To finish an interlock driveway or walkway, make sure that polymeric sand is used to fill in between the stones. Unlike natural sand, this product becomes almost like a rubberized mortar once it is sprayed down with water. Polymeric sand will prevent the stones from heaving from frost. And unlike dirt or natural sand, the sand discourages plant growth that can shift the stones. It also keeps ants and other bugs at bay. It will, however, wash away over time, so more must be swept into the cracks if gaps begin to form. That's the best way to protect the value of an interlocking hardscape.

The only other maintenance that is ordinarily required for an interlock (or natural stone) hardscape is a (usually) one-time washing. After natural or engineered stone has weathered for some time, it may produce a surface efflorescence or white stain. A stone cleaner is available to remove this, and usually only needs to be used once.

Hardscaping is more than just driveways and walkways, however. I like to add some three-dimensional elements to front and backyards, especially if there are elevation changes across the property. You can build retaining walls around an entire yard, or you can break up the height by terracing the yard. You can use small walls around raised flower beds or garden portions. And small pillars can be used to mark the entrance to a walkway or the base of a short flight of stairs. In higher-end neighbourhoods, landscaped stairs leading to a front door or a patio can also be a good investment. There are attractive engineered-stone products for these types of features, including capstones, setting stones and clips, so these can all be great DIY projects.

There are other ways to create retaining walls and pillars, of course. While poured concrete is still used by some people, it does have a tendency to snap and lean, and doesn't tend to look as timeless and stylish as engineered stone. And there was a period where people used reclaimed or new railway ties, but these are not going to get you any kind of return on investment. Natural wood will rot quickly, and the creosote used to preserve the reclaimed railway ties is a chemical most people want to avoid.

If you are using retaining walls and you have a drainage issue on your property, you should include a weeping tile system so you don't get ice buildups.

While I'm a big fan of engineered stone and interlock for hardscaping, natural stone can be a great addition for accents or small features. Large landscaping stones can add interest to a garden. Imported slate is stylish and can be affordable if you are using only a few larger stones.

LANDSCAPE LIGHTING

Landscape lighting—for example, spotlights on trees and shrubs, or lighting on walkways, retaining walls or pillars—can highlight some of the quality features of your home. But outdoor electrical work needs to be planned out. If you are doing an excavation or otherwise tearing up your yard, putting in the wiring for outdoor lighting can be an affordable add-on. But trying to retrofit lighting into a finished outdoor space can get very expensive and is not likely to give you much return on investment. That said, the cash outlay may provide benefits outside of resale value. Small lights on outdoor steps can improve the safety of your property. And outdoor lighting can address security and mobility issues. While motion-sensor lighting may improve visibility when you need it, lights that can be left on for extended periods do keep trespassers away. There are now adapters available, which hold light bulbs and can be screwed into fixtures, that can be set to keep a light on for a set number of hours or to turn a light on when darkness falls. They can also be programmed to turn the lights on and off at different times so that it looks as if someone is home. These may not add value for resale, but they can certainly add valuable security and peace of mind.

Backyards

SOFTSCAPING

As far as adding to your property's value, there are no particular rules or guidelines for plant choices or landscaping design. I know people who love lilac bushes and others who hate them. Some people will be delighted to find a mature apple tree in the back garden; others will think only of the work involved. So with back garden planting, you should pick what *you* like and what you feel you can maintain. That's really the key: what sort of a garden can you keep looking good? Generally, a lush, varied landscape, with different plants that bloom in each season, appeals to homebuyers. But if you can't keep the flower beds tidy and weed-free, and the bushes and trees healthy and well pruned, your heavily planted garden is not going to show well. If mowing and weeding the grass is all you can manage, then do that and keep the rest of the yard simple.

That being said, mature trees do tend to add to a property's perceived value. If you are moving into a newly built home, it might be smart to plant a tree or two in the backyard. Your best bet is a low-maintenance (versus fruit or chestnut), disease-resistant tree in a variety that can grow into a medium-height mature tree. Ask your local gardening centre for advice on what might work well in your growing zone. One more tree tip: plant large trees at the far end of your backyard, with smaller trees closer to your house.

HARDSCAPING

Decks

It used to be that decks were a bit of an afterthought when considering the value of a home. In other words, they were a nice extra, but certainly not something that would help get a higher price for a home at resale. That is simply not the case anymore. Decks are now a huge deal. While *Remodeling* magazine's 2013 Cost vs. Value Report suggests that decks can give you an ROI of 68 to 77 percent, I know that, if done wisely, they can return far more than that. After all, people have realized that decks actually add to the living space of a house. In other words, decks become outdoor "rooms," and people are equipping and furnishing them much as they would the rest of their home. You can now purchase outdoor sofas, coffee tables, dining sets, kitchens, bars and carpets.

So as long as the size and complexity of your deck (not to mention its cost) is appropriate to the overall value of your house, this home improvement is well worth doing—in fact, as far as return on investment, a wooden deck ranks right up there with kitchen remodels and new front doors!

I recommend that you spend somewhere between 2.5 and 5 percent of your house's total value on a deck, and under $10,000 on a 200-square-foot deck. (It's getting a little wacky if you spend more than that.) If possible, you want to have one part deck to five parts backyard. But if you have a tiny backyard (say, 10 feet by 10) and you want to make it all deck, I say go for it.

Even a small deck can add value to your home, but it should have space to hold a barbecue, a table and two to four chairs, which usually means a minimum of 100 square feet. Anything less is really a balcony and won't add the same value to your property. To maximize the value you are adding to your property, a deck should be in the 200-square-foot range. I also highly recommend that you provide lighting on your deck. Small, low-voltage post lights around the perimeter can provide enough illumination for you to navigate around the deck at night without having bright lights or spotlights from the house shining into the backyard. I also like to put a low-voltage light every few feet on any outdoor steps I have.

You should be able to enter your backyard from the deck. If you have poor grading in your backyard—in other words, steep sloping—a deck can resolve this by creating flat, usable space.

Before you build a deck, check on local building regulations. If a deck is more than 24 inches off the ground or fastened to the house, you may need a building permit. Likewise, if more than 99 square feet of it is enclosed, a permit may be necessary. There are also building codes for decks, like height restrictions for bleacher seats on the deck, height of railings, etc.

There are three types of material you can use for the deck boards. The least expensive option is pressure-treated wood. It's the most common choice, and in the first five years, it gives the best return on investment. (And it's used for the framing of most decks, regardless of the type of deck boards they feature.) But pressure-treated is also my least favourite. For starters, because this wood is chemically treated, you have to use gloves to handle it. I don't like the thought that I'm building a living space out of a material that is potentially toxic, especially in the first year or so. What's more, it needs a lot of maintenance. You need to let pressure-treated wood age for a year before you can stain it to allow the chemicals to leach out. In that time, it tends to get grey. And if you leave it unstained, it will certainly get grey and nasty-looking.

A composite deck costs more upfront, but doesn't require as much maintenance as cedar decking. Also, you can hide the fastening systems so you won't see screws or nails in the boards.

The second choice is cedar. Cedar looks great, is durable and can last a long time. But like any wood product, cedar requires considerable maintenance—cleaning, sanding and staining (and restaining). And it's about three times as expensive as pressure-treated wood. But cedar is extremely popular. It's often mentioned in real estate listings, and because it is the decking material of choice for most people, it will give you the best return on investment in the initial five to 10 years of a deck's life.

The third option, composite decking, is the most expensive (about three times as much as cedar), but for longevity and ease of care, it's my hands-down favourite, and it will give you the best ROI if you sell your home once the deck is 10 years or older. It's better looking than wood, as far as I'm concerned, and comes in a variety of styles (including distressed looks) and colours. The options are endless—you can do inlaid patterns or create interesting designs by changing up colours on borders, stairs or railings. And boards are available in all shapes—easily allowing you to build decks with eye-catching curves. Typically, composite decking is made from recycled material, saving trees and making it environmentally friendly. Best of all, the maintenance of composite decks couldn't be easier—no sanding or staining, just a once-a-year spring washing.

The construction of composite decks uses pressure-treated wood for the posts and the supporting structures. But there are hidden fastening systems available so you don't have to see nails or screws in the boards. And you won't get cupping or crowning of the boards the way you can with wood.

Composites have really evolved over the years, but there are still differences in quality (low-end composites are more likely to have defects). Composites should be guaranteed against warping, colour fade, rot, mould or mildew for 25 years, but the guarantee is only as good as the company that issues it. (The company needs to be around 25 years after you purchase the product to have that guarantee mean something!)

Of course, the big downside of composite decks is the price. And because of that high sticker price, you aren't going to get the ROI you would get from a cedar deck. This is one of those cases in which you have to weigh the personal advantages against the extra cost. The time saved on maintenance alone may make it worth the additional expense. And if you suspect you aren't going to find the time to do the necessary upkeep on a wooden deck, then your deck is not going to be a showpiece when you go to sell your house, and you are not likely to get as much money back on your investment. Spending the extra dollars up front for composite might have been worth it.

Fences

It can be very hard to get a lot of ROI on a fence (the AIC estimate for adding a wooden fence is 50 percent). That's partly because replacing a fence is really a maintenance project rather than a value-adding one. In a new neighbourhood, however, adding a fence may improve your home's value, if you can do it in an economical way.

The best way to keep fence costs down and return on investment as high as possible is to share the cost of the fence with your bordering neighbours. This works especially well in newly constructed neighbourhoods, when the neighbours can all get together, agree on a material and style, and negotiate with one contractor to do all the work for a discounted price. But even if you are working with only one neighbour, splitting costs is the best way to go. Sharing a fencing project also ensures that your fence can straddle the property line. If you are doing a fence on your own, your neighbour might insist on having the fence reside solely on your property.

There are a number of fencing materials that you can choose from. Pressure-treated wood is the most common. It can provide privacy and can be used in a number of different design styles. Chain-link is often used in older urban neighbourhoods with small lots. It offers no privacy but does keep small areas open to light and airflow. Wrought iron can be stylish but is typically seen only in high-end neighbourhoods or front gardens. Your best bet is to go with the neighbourhood standard. And check your municipal bylaws for fence-height requirements and restrictions before you build.

"Just for You" Hardscaping and Extras

These days, there are a lot of other relatively affordable extras you can add to your backyard. And while many of them will create an outdoor space that may well interest prospective homebuyers, most of these things fall under the "just for you" umbrella. Hot tubs, landscape lighting, outdoor fireplaces, outdoor kitchens, ponds or water features, and so on are all wonderful luxuries, but they are also items that require a fairly high level of maintenance. This will deter a segment of buyers who are not interested in those features (for instance, a pool).

Pergolas, Gazebos and Pavilions

Outdoor structures, like pergolas and gazebos, are popular these days, in part because it is so easy to find attractive, affordable prefab versions. But whether you opt for a DIY kit or a custom-built structure, you need to go for quality. If you choose one of the cheaper prefab models, it is not going to weather well and is likely to look really shabby in only a few years' time. And speaking of weather, anything too light can be blown over in the wind. There are quality products, however, available in a variety of building materials, including cedar, southern pine and pressure-treated wood. Because pergolas and gazebos don't usually get direct sun or the same kind of traffic that a deck gets, stained wood will last five to seven years before it needs to be refinished.

I recommend that you plan to put lighting in your pergola, gazebo or pavilion so that you can use the area for dining or other evening relaxation. You might also think of putting a fan in the roof of a gazebo or pavilion. An outdoor fan not only provides cooling during hot days and nights, but will also keep the bugs away.

In-Ground Irrigation Systems

In-ground irrigation systems for front and backyards are useful if you have a lot of space and a lot of planting. But they are very expensive and really only give any return on investment in higher-value homes.

Exterior DIYs

As mentioned throughout this chapter, there are a lot of good do-it-yourself projects around the exterior of your home. From gardening to hanging a new mailbox or putting up a privacy fence, a little labour on your part can go a long way towards improving your home's curb appeal and exterior features.

While softscaping can often be a DIY project, keep in mind that professional land-scapers often get a discount on plants, which can help if you hope to add a lot of trees, shrubs and pricier perennials. They can also install in-ground watering systems to ensure the health of your new garden. Most will provide a one-year warranty on plants and trees. If you do the landscaping yourself, make sure that you plan your plantings well so that they grow in over time but do not become too crowded. You should also provide a variety of plant heights to add dimensional interest to the garden and choose shrubs, trees and flowers so that something is in bloom during every season.

As far as hardscaping goes, small DIY projects might include building wooden planters, window boxes or small trellises and arbours. A privacy fence is also a good DIY project, although a full backyard fence is a much bigger job. Those with relatively high level DIY skills may want to tackle building a deck, but this is a big job too, and it needs to be done right—for aesthetics but, most important, for safety. If you do opt to do DIY projects that involve working with pressure-treated wood or cedar, keep in mind that the tannins in the wood make the sawdust very toxic if inhaled. Make sure that you wear a mask while cut-ting wood and that you work outdoors or in a very well-ventilated area.

Driveways and areas that get a great deal of foot traffic are hardscaping projects best left to professionals who have the tools and know-how to give you work that will remain serviceable and stay looking good for a long time. Laying a flagstone walkway or small patio, however, can be a do-it-yourself project, although the random shapes and depths of the stones make this a fiddly job. But as mentioned in my earlier discussions of hardscaping, today's engineered-stone products make small patios and walkways fairly straightforward DIY projects.

Using steel support structures for a second-storey deck instead of wood ones allowed us to create an additional outdoor room on the ground level of this backyard. We used composite planking, so the deck won't rot despite being under the trees.

Interlock Walkway

Materials needed: interlock paving stones, landscape fabric, gravel, sand, polymeric sand, metal edging and spikes.

Tools needed: shovel and rake, tamping tool and/or compacting machine, hammer, water supply and hose.

Make a plan of where you want your walkway to run and make a note of the measurements. Home reno or landscaping centres usually have displays that can give you plenty of ideas for walkway designs, patterns and stone choices. Keep in mind that if your design is very elaborate or involves curves, or if the stone shapes you want to use are not going to produce straight edges at the sides of your path, you will need to cut stone, which is a job for only very skilled do-it-yourselfers or professionals. For that reason, I am not providing instructions here for walkways with cut stones.

I use Permacon Trafalgar stone most often. It's an engineered-stone product that looks and performs as well as real stone but is manufactured to fit nicely together and to be level. Once you pick a stone pattern, you will need to calculate how many square feet of pavers you need. The reno or landscaping centre where you purchase the stone should be able to advise you of how much allowance you will need to build in to accommodate your walkway design and stone pattern. Usually, the interlock can be delivered to your home.

The first step to preparing the base for the pavers is to dig out the walkway to at least six inches plus the thickness of the stone (usually about eight inches). You want the stone at least an inch above the grass so that the water runs off it, and the stone must slope away from any structures, which usually means a 2 percent grade. You don't, however, have to dig this slope out. You can, instead, build it up with the fill.

After you have excavated your walkway site, line the ground under the walkway with a layer of landscape fabric to prevent weeds from growing up through your finished walkway stones.

If you are running your walkway from stairs to a driveway or sidewalk, you will want to grade the walkway from the steps to the sidewalk. Do the grading by posting stakes at either end of the walkway. Tie a string at the height on the stake at which you want the top of the paver to meet. Do the same at bottom. If the walkway is long or bends, you may need a stake at the middle where you place a mark at a height midway between the top and bottom heights of the path.

Next, pour your base. You have a couple of options for this fill material: pea gravel, gravel, or processed stone (a mixture of gravel and stone dust). You should have four inches of gravel for the base of a walkway and eight inches for a driveway. Create your 2 percent slope with this fill. Pack this base using a manual packing tool or motorized plate compactor (which you can rent from some landscaping or home-improvement centres), maintaining the 2 percent slope.

After the gravel has been thoroughly compacted, place two metal one-inch poles or pipes on the base material, near the edges of the path, so that they are at the height where the base of the interlock stones should be (with the string indicating where the top of the stones will be). Fill around these screed poles, between and at the sides, with sand or stone dust. Tamp down with a tamping tool or plate compactor. The sand should be slightly higher than, or level with, the tops of the poles.

Next, place a two-by-four board perpendicular to the poles, with each end of the board resting on a pole. Then pull the two-by-four along the poles and down the pathway until the sand is levelled out.

Lay the interlock stones in your pattern on top of this. Make sure you lower the stones carefully into place and don't drag them across the sand.

When you have finished laying the stones, place the metal edging securely along the sides of the path. Place the spikes into the holes provided, angling them slightly so that the bottoms of the spikes are pointing in towards the path. Drive in the spikes. (Once driven in, the spikes' ends will be slightly angled below the stones.) Next, pour polymeric sand over the entire area of the pavers, sweeping it into the gaps between the stones. When the gaps are completely filled, sweep off the excess. Tamp or compact the pavers again, and then spray the polymeric sand down with a bit of water. Allow the sand to dry, and then repeat the wetting process.

Chapter 8

INCOME SUITES

What's the best way to add significant value to your home? Income suites, hands down! A legal income suite increases the value of a home in a number of ways. First, adding an attractive, well-kept apartment can increase your home's resale price, particularly in an overheated market. When housing prices are high, the income the purchaser can make will mean that your property is affordable to more people. In fact, banks consider legal rental suites as qualifying income, which often turns non-approved or marginal buyers into mortgage-qualified ones. And that means more bids for the home seller, which in turn means a higher selling price. But even if you are not selling right away, you can see immediate benefits to the rental suite. The income it generates can reduce your mortgage and increase your equity. (And since the bank considers this rent to be additional income, your mortgage ratio is lower—increasing your ability to borrow to invest in other properties if you wish.) Rental income can also allow you to hold on to a home in order for it to appreciate in value. (And actually, that's the traditional principle at play in real estate investment: income properties largely pay for themselves as the unit increases in value over time.)

Properties with separate apartments in them have really broadened their appeal in recent years. Demographic studies have shown more and more people are moving into the cities. Housing prices tend to be higher in urban areas—and are becoming more so with the urbanization of our population. For many people looking for housing in the city, therefore, the affordable answer is either a condo or a house with an income suite in it. And as the population moves to the city, houses with income suites carry less and less risk because the demand for rental units is also on the rise.

Income suites really shine in an urban environment and in cities with colleges and universities. Homes with rental suites always sell for more in a university town—that's where I started my income property investments, and I still own a large number of houses in these areas. In suburban areas, income suites aren't quite as popular as in the big city, although they are doing well there too. But not every market is good for rental properties. Homes in very high-end areas are likely to feature "nanny" suites instead of rental accommodations. And if you live in an area where there is high unemployment and poor public transportation, the potential to rent out an income suite in your home may be limited.

But even for people who aren't looking for income potential, houses with separate apartments in them are becoming increasingly popular. A significant slice of our population belong to the "sandwich generation"—taking care of children, but also taking care of aging parents. Multi-unit homes can be a perfect way to keep several generations of a family together—whether it is elderly parents or adult children who are not yet able to afford their own living spaces. If you are thinking of renovating your home to accommodate your extended family, the best way is to create a separate legal apartment. That way, when it's time to sell, your property will appeal to both families like yours and to those who are interested in a house that can be a home and generate some rental income.

As I said at the beginning of the chapter, income suites are a great way to add value to your home. But like all investments, there are risks as well as rewards. The rewards are pretty obvious: cheques to the bank! But you have to be willing to do a bit of extra work to earn that extra money. You can't cut corners here. If you do, the income suite and landlord-tenant relationship is going to be a difficult process and a disaster in the long run. You've got to be ready to be a landlord and to acknowledge that some of your house is now the personal space of other people. Of course, you should always maintain your home so that you can live comfortably and see your house's value increase. But when you have tenants, you also have an obligation to them to keep your entire home clean, safe and properly maintained. For a number of people, it isn't the idea of maintenance as much as the thought of having strangers living under their roof that is off-putting. The truth, however, is that the rules and regulations that apply to the design of income suites create spaces that are truly separate—living in a house with an income suite is like living in a condo or a semi-detached home.

And once you've accepted the responsibility of being a landlord and managing and maintaining an income suite, you need to do some legwork to assess whether this move will be a financially feasible and advantageous one for you. What kind of rental accommodation is already available in your area, and what rents are these places charging? What is your current financial situation? Do you have the money to invest in quality renovations? If not, can you borrow the money at a reasonable rate? When homeowners are considering a loan in order to create an income suite, I always suggest that they borrow only as much as they can pay back with two to five years of rental income. Two years is really ideal, but house and reno costs have risen over the years, so that benchmark may be hard to achieve in certain markets. Even if it takes you up to five years to pay off the loan, you are still making money, but longer than that, it may not make financial sense to become a landlord. And even if you have cash at your disposal for the necessary renovations, you need to weigh the cost of creating the income suite against the revenue it will produce and the appreciation of the value of the home. There may be some housing markets where you just aren't going to be getting a decent ROI with income suites. (Check out my books *Cash Flow for Life* and *Quick Start to Cash Flow* for more information about financial planning for income properties by visiting www. lifetimewealthacademy.com.)

Assessing the Potential

If you decide that adding an income suite to your home is a good financial move for you, the next thing you have to do is assess whether the house you have (or the one you are considering purchasing) actually has the potential to accommodate a separate apartment—not all do. Some spaces might be renovated to allow for an income suite, but at a cost that is just too high to make it worthwhile. And even if the layout and space seem adequate, can an income suite be built that meets municipal bylaws and building codes so that the apartment is legal?

Every municipality has bylaws for multi-unit homes, but these bylaws will vary. In fact, in some municipalities, bylaws have been introduced that forbid income suites in family homes. Places that tend to restrict income suites are typically suburban areas that want to maintain their low population density or places that want to encourage more new construction and therefore more property tax potential. In Ontario, however, all municipalities need to allow income suites. But to further complicate things, some municipalities will allow "secondary suites" for extended family use only, or for limited periods of time, or only in certain

In this basement income suite, we used the support post as a visual anchor for the kitchen and the high-end range hood as a statement piece for the entire space. While the rest of the reno is modest, the overall result will attract quality tenants.

More About the Numbers

While you need to accurately assess how much it will cost to build an income suite and what revenues you might expect to get, there are a few other numbers that should figure into your financial considerations.

- Your property tax may be raised slightly to reflect your home's increased value after you've put in the income suite.
- The income that the suite generates is not only considered income by the banks (and therefore increases your ability to borrow) but also by the Canada Revenue Agency. The additional income tax you may have to pay, however, can be offset by deductions for the operating costs of the unit (a portion of your utility costs, property tax, maintenance and repair costs, and so on).
- If you are building or renovating an income suite in a property that is not your home, you may be able to write off these costs against future capital gains. Always check with your accountant about what expenses can be claimed and what revenues need to be reported.
- Your home insurance costs may rise to cover the change in your home's value and the fact that you have additional people living on the property, but usually this is not a significant increase. You can, however, add a rider that will protect you against loss of rental income if something like a flood should make the unit unfit for renting for a time. But you will pay a premium for this.
- Your homeowner's insurance cannot cover your tenant's possessions. You need to let your tenants know that they will need their own insurance.
- If you don't have the utilities on separate meters, you will likely see an increase in your gas, electrical and water bills. If you pay for garbage pickup (or for the large sizes of garbage cans provided by your city), make sure you add this to the costs of doing business.

kinds of houses or buildings (say, completely detached homes or in accessory buildings, like a garage), or only when limited to a certain size or to a certain number of rooms. Before you embark on any plans, check with your municipality to find out what zoning bylaws and income suite bylaws apply to your neighbourhood. As far as I'm concerned, ignoring the bylaws that govern income suites and creating an apartment that isn't legal just isn't worth it. You may very well get busted by the city if it's discovered that you are operating outside the law, and an illegal income suite will not increase the resale price of your home. (If you are shopping for a home with income potential, this is something to keep in mind: not all existing income suites are actually legal, and many may not have the potential to be converted into legal spaces.)

Up until about 1990, most provincial building codes didn't have specific rules for income suites in primary dwellings. Any "apartments" fell under the regulations for duplexes and small apartment buildings—where the requirements were extremely rigorous and usually expensive to provide. Since then, a number of provincial building codes have introduced sections that govern new building of family homes that feature secondary suites as well as renovations that add these units to existing homes. Alberta has been at the forefront of these building code revisions, but other provinces are following suit. To get a clear sense of what your home or one you are considering purchasing needs to have in place to create a legal income suite, you really need to check the provincial building codes. But in general, you should be looking for the following elements:

- Basements or extra space that was undeveloped when the house was built.
- Adequate ceiling heights. Whether in a basement or an attic space, ceilings must have seven feet of clearance over 75 percent of the space. Beneath bulkheads and sloped roofs, some of the space can go down to 6½ feet, but this reduced height can cover only 25 percent of the total space. You can dig out basements to give you more height, but this is a costly measure (about $300 per linear foot) and usually blows the renovation budget.
- A separate entrance. Any legal income suite is going to need its own separate entrance (and an additional point of egress—but more about that later). In most cases, a separate entrance is just too expensive to add, so this is something that may very well determine whether a property has income potential or not. A separate entrance might be a side door that leads to staircases down to a basement or up to a second floor (and perhaps to the main floor as well). Another way a separate

entrance can be created is with a front-hall entrance that opens to stairs that go up or down to the floor where the rental unit will be located. Often these entrance areas can be partitioned so that they accommodate two or more doors that lead to the separate areas of the house. Keep in mind that an entrance to the basement that requires the tenant to pass through another area of the house (the garage, for instance) does not constitute a separate entrance.

If you have these three elements in place, you're laughing. Just about everything else you will need to make a legal income unit can be added during the renovation.

Some styles of homes lend themselves more easily to income suites than others. Bungalows are ideal for basement units, as the space below grade is generally equal to the space on the main floor (and bungalows often have big footprints because all the living space happens on one level). Sidesplits and backsplits work well too because they usually have multiple entrances and a number of possible ways that space can be divided.

Space in fully detached homes is easier to convert into separate units than that in semi- or fully attached homes because windows can be located on any side (a help if windows need to be added to the income suite) and because some of the other things required by various municipal bylaws are easier to add in a detached home. And three-storey homes (many of which are from the Victorian era) often lend themselves well to income suites; the floor sizes tend to be generous, and above-grade apartments (third floor, for example, as opposed to basement units) always demand higher rents (although they do not add more to the property value than below-grade units). What's more, many three-storey houses feature a staircase that leads right to the front door. This makes it easy to close off the stairway on the railing side to create separate entrances on each level.

Finally, any house that has a separate building on site, like a coach house or a garage, has great potential for income suites. While apartments can be built above attached garages, a detached garage has the advantages of a detached house, and a suite above it can have the windows and light that bring higher rents.

But the key to creating an income suite in any house is the divisibility of the space. I've added rental units in all sorts of homes, but some are easier to create than others. I only rule out building income suites if the resulting unit can't be made legal, costs too much to build or will result in an apartment that is awkwardly laid out or just plain subpar. It all comes back to that fundamental principle of income properties: quality tenants make income suites work, and quality space attracts quality tenants!

The Design

The first thing you need to do once you've decided to go ahead with an income suite is to get plans drawn up and approved by the city. And this is a step that you want to get right. Designing any kind of living space requires planning and vision, but putting a whole apartment into a limited space in an existing dwelling presents some real challenges. The key here is not to overwhelm yourself with the endless number of options. I usually try to come up with two logical layout choices that present the most functional, practical use of the space while accommodating the homeowners' needs as well.

To achieve that, the first thing I do is determine where the main entrance to the apartment is going to be. There may be an existing entrance that will work (that does not require the tenant to pass through other parts of the house or the garage)—if so, that's great. If there isn't a suitable existing entrance, I figure out where I can build one.

Then I move on to the placement of the kitchen and bathroom. These are the toughest to design and build, as they involve plumbing, electrical, cabinets and other permanent fixtures. They also need a minimum ceiling height to accommodate cabinets and showers.

KITCHEN AND LIVING SPACE

I like to put the kitchen and main living space as close to the main entrance as possible. Income suites are usually condensed units, and you want to maximize space as much as you can. There isn't a lot of value to a large foyer in an apartment. I also like to combine kitchen and living space so that I have an open concept for the public rooms. This gives the unit a feeling of more space, but it also means that the area can share all the windows, which helps with the window requirements (see page 167 for more on windows in rental units). If you need to add a window, you can do that in the living room and not take up kitchen wall space that you might want to use for cupboards.

The plumbing and the existing plumbing stack usually determine what side of the space

(continues on page 162)

Here's proof that you can pack a lot of living space into a very small area. The island provides both counter space and seating, while the moulding-adorned support posts define the dining area. The white upper cabinets create the illusion of height, while the cascading countertop on the island creates visual interest.

This is what I call a "recycled" income suite. Since we were working on a tight budget, we painted the existing wall panelling and stained and refinished the parquet floors. We moved existing kitchen cabinets from another part of the house and painted them, but left some of the doors off to create a display look. We used the money we saved here on quality touches, like the island, shelf brackets, faucets and furniture.

is best for the kitchen. (The best way to limit the costs of renovations? Don't move too much plumbing!) In an income suite, you don't want to take up too much space with the kitchen. Therefore, you usually can't consider oversized appliances, and even the standard-sized appliances that you might have in the rest of the house might eat up too much room. If space is limited, consider smaller appliances. You can go with a 24-inch fridge and an oven of the same width (instead of the standard 30- or 36-inch models). You can also opt for a 24-inch sink base, with cupboards above it. You'll want a bank of drawers at least 12 inches wide and another 24-inch base cabinet for storage. If you have the room, you can add a dishwasher, and if space is tight, go with a smaller unit 18 inches wide. A peninsula or island can provide extra counter space, either for working or eating. You can buy prefab rolling islands on castors, but any other kinds of cabinets need to be fixed to the floor so that they don't tip. You also need to make sure that the cabinets, walls and work areas of the kitchen are wired, so that you don't have extension cords crossing the room.

You'll want to read about lighting in the chapter on kitchens while drawing up your income suite plans, but keep in mind that lighting in a basement income suite will largely be recessed in the form of pot lights. This is particularly true in high-traffic areas, like the kitchen, because of the limited ceiling heights of most basements.

The narrow island in this galley kitchen both defines the space and makes it feel twice as big. Despite its small size, this kitchen has everything you need.

And just like the kitchen in the main unit of the house, your income suite kitchen should have a good-quality range hood for ventilation. In basement suites, it is particularly important that the range hood vent outside to reduce cooking odours and moisture.

As with any kind of house, condo or apartment, a nice kitchen makes a huge difference in the appeal of the unit. The key is to make the kitchen look high-end without spending the "high-end" bucks.

BATHROOM

The ideal location for the bathroom is off of a hallway that leads to a bedroom or off the main living space. Given that income units are usually pretty compact spaces, try to avoid putting the bathroom too close to the kitchen, for privacy and hygiene reasons.

If space permits, you should provide a four-piece bathroom in a rental unit. This is particularly important if your income suite can accommodate a family. A three-piece bathroom with a luxurious shower might, however, work well for an executive suite.

The standard bathroom design and dimensions as described in chapter 3 are really ideal for any rental units. So a room five feet wide can have the tub across the back wall, with a 24-inch vanity on one side and a 36-inch space between the edge of the bathtub and the edge of the vanity to accommodate the toilet. You don't need to have a window in a bathroom, but ventilation is very important, especially in a basement unit. In fact, even if there is a window in the bathroom space, I recommend installing a high-quality fan, as moisture is a real issue in a basement apartment. A fan is the best way to combat moisture buildup. And even if there is a window, many people don't like to open windows in basement apartments. (Being high up on the wall, they can be difficult to get at, and anyone walking by can see into them.) Frankly, I usually try to avoid having a window in a bathroom at all. Not only don't they serve ventilation purposes well, but they also need to be vinyl windows, properly sealed (especially when they are in a shower area, which they usually are when they are in a bathroom). Even then, all of the seams and crevices are real mould and mildew magnets.

And because you really want to guard against excess moisture in a basement unit, I almost always tile the bathroom floors. Another thing I love to do with the floors of income suite bathrooms is install in-ground heating. Basement floors can be cold, so it's a logical choice if the unit is below grade. But even if the rental unit is on the second or third floor, in-floor heating can save you space (for rads) or eliminate the need to run extra ductwork to the bathroom. Check out the discussion of heated floors on p. 73.

Just like in the main living space of a house, the bathroom in a rental unit can have a huge impact on the value of the space—in this case, to prospective tenants. While I usually don't go for the most high-end tiles or fixtures on the market, I do generally opt for a little luxury in this room. I try to go with modern, stylish hardware and fixtures, glass shower doors and good-quality floor tiles. I also like to put those heated towel bars in income suite bathrooms. Tenants get so excited by this little touch of luxury—which suggests not just a quality unit but also a landlord who is committed to making the space truly pleasant for his or her tenants.

BEDROOMS

The size and placement of bedrooms are fairly straightforward. You want the main bedroom to be as far away from the kitchen and the main entrance as possible. Your local building codes for rental units will tell you the minimum size required, but you always want to have enough room for a bed (ideally a queen-size bed in the master or only bedroom) and a couple of nightstands. You will also want to have space for a closet. And in order to market a room as a bedroom, it *must* have a window. If it doesn't, it can only legally be listed as an office or additional space. That may be a marketing feature, but it won't allow you to capitalize on the rent.

Basement Windows

Windows in basements can rob the occupants of some privacy because it's relatively easy for anyone at street level to peer in. For this reason, you will want to make sure that basement bathrooms have windows with frosted glass. There may also be other areas of basement family rooms or apartments (like sleeping areas) where frosted glass might be desirable. You can order windows with opaque glass of various styles, replace the glass of existing windows, or buy film to transform the existing glass. While you can buy "peel and stick" films for windows, I prefer ones that are applied with water and a trowel to push out bubbles. The key to these types of film is to cut it slightly larger than the glass itself, as the film tends to shrink as it dries on the window.

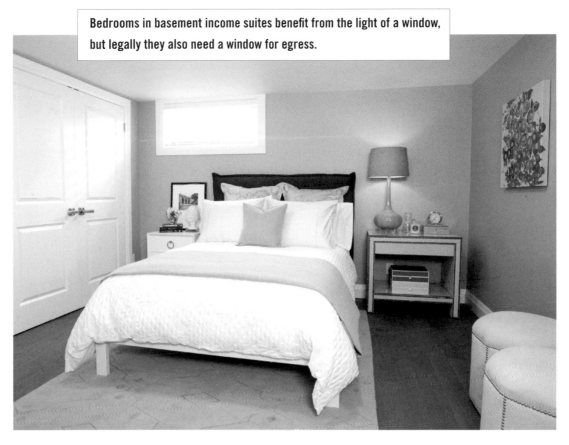

Bedrooms in basement income suites benefit from the light of a window, but legally they also need a window for egress.

But how many bedrooms should you try to get into your income suite? If you are targeting your income suite to the student market, more bedrooms can mean more rent. Two or three bedrooms also mean that your income suite may appeal to families. But if you have to make the bedrooms really small, the unit isn't likely to appeal to either of these groups—in which case, you'd be better off with one large, comfortable bedroom instead of two cramped ones. At least one bedroom should be able to accommodate a queen-size bed. I've had the most success with one-bedroom units (which are preferred by professionals or couples) and three-bedroom suites that work for parents and children. One word of advice: don't opt for a single bedroom because you want only one tenant. Keep in mind that most people don't stay single forever, so that one bedroom is likely to be occupied by two people sooner or later.

If you do design your income suite with two or more bedrooms, you need to think about the separation between them. The best way to create a sound buffer between two rooms is to have the shared wall house the closets.

FRONT ENTRANCES

As mentioned above, there isn't usually room in an income suite for much of a foyer. In an ideal scenario, however, you would have space to add a small closet or wardrobe near the main entrance that can store shoes and coats. Keep in mind that storage is important to renters as well as homeowners—often more important than landlords realize. It's a good idea to do what you can to build in as much storage space as possible when drawing up the design for your rental unit.

OTHER SOURCES OF EGRESS

Income suites always need a second source of egress if the main entrance is shared (not a dedicated egress for the unit). This second source of egress will provide an escape route if the main entrance is blocked. If you're lucky, you may have a shared entranceway (say, a side door that leads to the entrance to the main living space as well as to the rental unit). If there isn't a second entrance, a window can serve as the alternative source of egress, as long as it is big enough. If you don't have a window that will serve this function, you will have to add or enlarge an existing window. An egress window typically needs to have an opening of five square feet, with height or width no shorter than 18 inches. The base of this window needs to be no more than three feet from the floor. If the base is any higher than this, there needs to be a ladder or a fixed piece of furniture (like a kitchen countertop) beneath it to serve as access to the window. If the window is above grade, great. If not, the window well outside needs to extend at least three feet from the side of the house. And any egress windows need to open without the use of tools. Finally, some provincial building codes require there to be a window that can be used as an exit in *each* bedroom.

OTHER DESIGN TIPS

When you are looking to maximize your return on investment—whether it's on a home sale or an apartment rental—remember that the design and decoration of your space should appeal to 90 percent of the population 90 percent of the time. But you also need to give yourself a bit of an edge. To be honest, when it comes to rental units, most on the market are poorly maintained. You want to make sure yours isn't one of these, but simply being a well-maintained space is not necessarily going to make your place anyone's first choice. The best way to put your unit on the top of everyone's list is to provide one design element that attracts people's attention and hooks them on your space, something that makes your unit more attractive than all of the other places they've looked at. This could be anything from a fancy backsplash or stylish piece of cabinetry in the kitchen to a living room wall with striking wallpaper or a gas fireplace. You want to add something that creates an impact very quickly once people have entered the apartment—so features in the kitchen or living area work best. If there is a large entrance or hallway in the unit, this might be another place to create the "wow" factor. But don't overdo it. One great element that gives your unit personality is enough.

And finally, you can certainly do the design yourself, but if you have any doubts or know that this is not your strong suit, by all means hire a qualified designer or an architect who has had experience designing income suites. It's important to get the design of your income suite right if you want to make it work for you as well as your tenants.

Construction and Building Requirements

In most municipalities and counties, there are very few—or no—rules for multigenerational homes or homes with nanny suites, in-law suites or other sorts of shared living arrangements. A house with these sorts of divisions is simply considered a family home and doesn't have a higher value on the resale market. A *legal* income suite, one that meets all of the zoning and building codes in your area, will get you that higher price. Meeting all of those design and construction requirements may cost you about 25 percent more than standard renovations to "finish" a basement, but the extra expenditure will be worth it in the long run, as it will significantly raise your home's value on resale.

WINDOWS

Each building zone will have guidelines about the number of windows a rental unit must have. Usually, you don't need windows in bathrooms, laundry rooms, mechanical rooms or offices. You do need windows in kitchens, living rooms and bedrooms. (And in some provinces, these bedroom windows have to have openings large enough to act as sources of egress, as described above.)

Windows are required in income suites for light, ventilation and egress. Typically, the windows need to account for five square feet of each room.

In this main-floor apartment, the double doors allow light into the windowless bedroom and create an open feel in a compact space.

Careful planning of any renovation, especially basements, is worth the time and expense.

FIRE SEPARATION

The number one concern of building inspectors, fire departments and (hopefully) the home-owners and tenants is that, in a property with more than one living space, one unit doesn't compromise the safety of the other. The primary issue here is smoke and fire. A number of steps need to be taken to ensure that smoke, heat and flames don't travel easily from one unit to the other in the event of a fire.

When constructing an income unit, the vertical walls between side-by-side units are built to serve as fire separation; in stacked units, the separation is incorporated into the ceiling and floor construction.

Walls and ceilings can be framed with standard joists, but these need to be filled with Roxul or another rock wall product. (This insulation serves as fire protection *and* sound insulation.) I use two layers, as long as they can fit in loosely—forcing or compacting the insulation reduces its effectiveness. On top of the insulation and joists goes $^5/_8$-inch Type-X fire-resistant, fire-rated drywall (also called gypsum). The drywall must be taped and mudded thoroughly—there can't be any gaps or cracks in the drywall, as the seal must be complete to prevent smoke migration. If space permits, some builders will construct walls and ceilings with two layers of drywall for an even stronger barrier between units. The walls and ceilings of the furnace room—even if they are not part of the income suite—need to be $^5/_8$-inch drywall as well. (Remember to check the building codes in your area to confirm that the specifications above meet all of the requirements.)

Of course, a ceiling is going to have breaks in the drywall for lights and vents. So any pot lights need to be fire rated, and the space around the lights has to be well insulated. Special vents with fire dampers are also advisable. These vents have a metal plate in the duct that is tied back with a soldered spring. When the spring gets hot, the solder melts, allowing the plate to swing down, sealing the duct. These fire damper vents are only about $15 and well worth the money.

If your suite involves new construction, another great option is to go with fire-rated plumbing. I use System 15 plumbing. Marginally more expensive than standard PVC or ABS plumbing, it is grey (versus white or black) and has a higher melting point so it doesn't melt as fast as standard pipes and prevents fire from breaching the separation of the two units.

You will also need fire-rated doors between the two units and in shared areas. Typically, you need doors that have 20-minute fire ratings—these are usually solid-core ones. (The fire rating indicates how many minutes the door can withstand fire before being breached.) These doors are available in standard sizes at building centres, but custom sizes can also be special-ordered. The hardware on these doors—knobs, locks and self-closing hinges—also has to be fire-rated. And always insulate around door jambs with an extra bit of Roxul.

SMOKE ALARMS

When you have more than one living unit in a property, you must have interconnected smoke alarms so that if one goes off in one unit, the alarms in other units will also sound. (Don't count on hearing an alarm in another unit. If the sound insulation between the units has been done well, you might not notice the noise.) Even better than interconnected smoke alarms are combined interconnected smoke and carbon monoxide detectors. These will usually have to be wired in, although there are now wireless interconnected smoke alarms. If you go wireless, you may have to wire in separate carbon monoxide detectors. And depending on the provincial building codes for secondary suites, you may need to have one smoke alarm no more than 5 metres (16 feet, 3 inches) from each bedroom.

While there are many quality products out there, I usually opt for Kidde alarms, as they've been the most reliable and have the longest battery life, in my experience.

You should also add in-duct smoke alarms or in-duct shut-off relays—sensors that are connected to the furnace and shut it off when they sense smoke in the ductwork.

SOUND INSULATION

The number one reason tenants leave a rental space is noise. And the most common complaint of homeowners with income suites is sound transfer. No one wants to hear others or wants to think that their daily lives can be overheard by their neighbours. Indeed, noise creates tension between residents—the less they hear of each other, the more they like each other. With proper sound insulation between units, you can make sure that everyone can have the quiet and privacy they want.

"Sound transfer classification" is a system that calculates the amount of sound that has been reduced between two units. Ideally, you want an STC of 50 or greater; in other words, you want to block out 50 percent or more of the noise moving between one unit and another.

As mentioned above, the fire- and smoke-proofing insulation of ceilings and walls is also an excellent method of absorbing airborne noises—mid-tone sounds like voices, dogs' barking, TV and music. I always try to get two layers of Roxul into walls and ceilings. I also like to put layers of Roxul between the interior walls of a rental space. Income suites tend to be compact spaces, so sound insulation can provide a measure of privacy for people living in close quarters. (This is especially useful in units with more than one tenant.) Also, if you can reduce the noise transfer *within* an apartment, you will also be reducing the noise transfer *between* units.

For stacked units, decoupling systems reduce the noise that transfers from the floor of one unit and the ceiling of another. These systems are composed of resilient or furring channels made of metal, which run perpendicular to the ceiling joists of the lower unit, creating a cushion between the joists and the drywall. The channels dissipate the vibrational noise of footsteps, stereo bass and the movement of furniture before this sound can reach the drywall. Thicker drywall can help absorb vibrational noise as well, as can special floor assemblies. For example, a Schluter mat or decoupling membrane can be installed between the subfloor and tile of the upper unit. This kind of decoupling membrane can also help prevent cracking and heaving of the tile by allowing the subfloor to move or shift beneath the tile, while the tile stays put.

Special attention should also be paid to the floor coverings of both upper and lower units. In an upper unit, the right flooring will reduce the amount of noise travelling to the lower unit. In a lower unit, sound-absorbing floors will stop noise from bouncing off the floor onto the hard ceiling above. A carpet and a good underpad, even if they aren't wall to wall, can provide a huge amount of sound dampening. The better engineered-hardwood products allow a soundproofing mat to be laid underneath the floating hardwood and above the concrete pad—something to bear in mind in a lower unit. Remember, anything you can do to reduce noise in *both* units will help reduce sound transfer, and therefore noise, in each of them.

As with fire separation, some builders like to add a double layer of drywall for additional insulation. While Roxul acts as a sound absorber, an extra layer of drywall will act as a sound deflector.

ELECTRICAL

The wiring requirements for an income suite are the same as for a family home (see chapter 5 for more on this), but if you are doing a whole-house reno or rewiring job, it makes sense to put each unit on a separate panel, with a separate meter. This way, homeowners and tenants can be responsible for their own utilities. If, however, you are restricting your renos to the income suite and are doing new electrical work in this area, I suggest that you run the wiring for the rental unit to its own pony, or subpanel, so that your tenants have their own breakers.

HVAC

Unless you are adding an income suite to some unheated area of the house (building a space on top of the garage, for example, or opening up an attic), your current furnace is likely to be sufficient for both units (calculations that have determined what size furnace your home needed would have taken into account the basement or second-floor space). But if you are adding a lot of windows or rearranging ductwork, you may need to get an engineer to do a heat-loss calculation for your home and determine the revised needs for your new house design. When building your income unit, the ideal scenario is to place all heating registers at ground level so that the heat rises. In basements, this means having the ducts at the base of the walls (with the ductwork running down the walls). If you aren't planning to do a lot of ductwork, it is okay to leave the registers in the ceiling, where they would normally be. Frankly, I prefer to work with existing ductwork. Those heat-loss calculations can be expensive, and moving ductwork requires a separate HVAC permit, so I like to avoid that if possible. (But check your provincial and municipal building codes. Some require separate heating and ventilation systems for new homes being built with income suites or with any new construction of an income suite.)

PLUMBING

Adding a mixing valve on a water heater, which adds a bit of cold water to the hot water leaving the tank (and which usually costs about $75) is a good idea for any homeowner, but if you have an income suite, this may be mandatory in your area. Even if it isn't, you shouldn't think about doing this. It will protect your family and your tenants from being scalded by hot water—and protect you from liability.

I also recommend adding shut-off valves to all of the plumbing fixtures in your house. This way, if work has to be done on any of these things, water does not have to be shut off in the other unit(s). Most people will add shut-off valves to sinks and toilets, but it is also important to have them on showers, washers, laundry tubs and dishwashers.

HANDRAILS

Handrails for staircases with more than two steps are a requirement in pretty much all parts of the country. Frankly, this building code is not always enforced, but if you forgo railings, it could turn into a liability issue for you. As a landlord, I feel it is always best to protect myself as well as my tenants, so I don't skimp on the handrails.

A Few Other Income Suite Hints

I typically rent the hot water heaters, furnaces and air conditioning units in my rental properties. That way, if a problem arises, my tenants can call the company that owns the units for service without going through me. If the rental unit is in your home, you wouldn't rent these items.

As anyone who knows me or has seen my show knows, I'm obsessed with adding value to homes. So income suites really get me going. But not only does the suite itself increase a house's value—the kind of major renovation needed to add one is a fantastic opportunity to up the ante and increase your home's value outside of the suite itself. If you've got walls or ceilings down during the suite's construction, why not take advantage of that by updating wiring, plumbing and HVAC for the rest of the house? It won't raise the value of the suite, but the work will raise the value of your home (see chapter 5 for more on this).

Adding an income suite is not a quick or inexpensive renovation, and it has to be done in a timely fashion so that you can start collecting those cheques and reaping some of the ROI as soon as possible. But you can't cut corners with this kind of reno completion. While any changes you make to your main house can be done over any length of time that works for you, you don't have the same luxury with an income suite. If you rent out the unit with only 90 percent of the work done, are you willing to accept only 90 percent of the rent? Even if you are willing to reduce the rent, an unfinished apartment is going to draw complaints from your renters, and may even lose you great tenants.

And a final note about rental suites: on my TV show, *Income Property*, when we've finished renovating or creating the apartments, many of the homeowners find themselves wanting to move into the new space instead of giving it to their tenants. The quality finishes, the bright, fresh decor, the well-designed space are a real draw—even for the homeowner. (The most common compliment I get about below-grade units is "This doesn't feel

Tip: If you feel that you need outside help (perhaps to find tenants for very expensive or high-end rentals), I recommend hiring a professional property manager over rental locators at real estate agencies. Real estate agencies are focused on selling properties; the rental market will always be an afterthought for them. And agents take a fee for every tenant they place in a property, and then they walk away. So they don't have a lot of incentive to find the right tenant for your property. Property managers, by contrast, get a cut of every month's rent, so they benefit if the tenant-landlord relationship is long and healthy. But remember, any outside help will eat into your rental income, so it's worth thinking twice before signing on managers or agents.

like a basement at all!") And that is sometimes partly due to the fact that the new space is more updated and luxurious than the main residence. This will seem a bit odd or a bit counterintuitive to some people. They might think, "Why would I put a nicer kitchen faucet in my income suite than the one I have in my own kitchen? Why put a heated towel rack in the apartment bathroom if I don't have one?" The answer is simple: *the quality of the space dictates the quality of the tenant.* And great tenants will be easy to live with, will take care of your property (and therefore your investment) and will bring you those nice big cheques each and every month. And those cheques mean that you will eventually be able to afford a new kitchen faucet—or whole new kitchen—for yourself! So make sure your income suite matches the quality of your own living space—or exceeds it. It will pay off for you in the long run.

Finding Great Tenants

Adding an income suite is a fantastic way to increase the value of your home, but it's a big investment and so should be protected. The best way to do that is by having tenants who will keep the suite clean and in good condition. But how do you find those great tenants? My advice is to be proactive. Don't rely on luck. Instead, put yourself in the driver's seat when searching for tenants and when interacting with them when they move in. That is the best way to keep things running as smoothly as possible.

THE CALIBRE OF YOUR SPACE DICTATES THE CALIBRE OF YOUR TENANT

Never discount the fact that there are great tenants out there looking for great places! Typically, the better the condition your place is in, the easier it will be to rent. With a high-calibre property, tenants will be willing to pay more, will stay longer and will be less likely to miss a payment because they don't want to lose the place.

Features that most tenants look for include:

1. safety—an apartment that is in good, safe working order;
2. cleanliness;
3. a modern space—updated layout, appliances and decor;
4. new floors.

These four expectations are not difficult to meet, and slightly exceeding them will make your space the cream of the crop!

ADVERTISING AND MARKETING

Strong marketing makes it easy to find great tenants. And the best way—hands down—to advertise your property is on Internet rental sites. The reasons? Unlike newspapers, online listings have a longer shelf life. (They aren't going to be lining the cat box the day after they appear.) And unlike print ads or traditional bulletin boards, online rental sites allow you to post plenty of pictures—always worth a thousand words, as they say. But even more important than shelf life and photos, savvy renters tend to check online for listings rather than scouring through the tattered ads on grocery store or laundromat bulletin boards.

You can use Craigslist or Kijiji, but targeted sites are usually more effective. Most cities have local rental search engines. Many areas also have rental search engines geared to students, and some universities and colleges offer online off-campus rental listings.

Other than photos, what information should you put in your ad? Make sure you state the availability date of your rental—the first of the month is the most popular move-in time. And go ahead and boast about the strengths of your property—its location, size, appliances, parking, laundry and amenities, as well as other selling points like brightness, neighbourhood and proximity to public transportation. Your ad should also prepare prospective clients with realistic expectations: if utilities are not included or there is an additional fee for parking, for example, be up front about that.

When preparing your ad, always check out the competition. Spending time looking at other ads for properties in your area will give you a good idea of what rental units similar to yours are going for. And note the way in which other property owners describe the neighbourhood. You can also see the differences between listings that are aimed at students, at families and at single renters. If you find ads that really grab your attention, feel free to copy them. No need to reinvent the wheel!

Once you've got the move-in date, rent and description down, pick a date for showings and state it in the ad. I find it works best to set aside several hours (say, 9 A.M. to 12 noon) for all showings, so that I can control my schedule. But don't provide an address for an "open house"—that will only result in a confusing free-for-all. Instead, ask people to book an appointment for a time during that showing period. I schedule my appointments close together—15 minutes apart for family-sized apartments, five to 10 minutes for tours of smaller units. This might sound a bit hectic, but it works well for two reasons. First, there are always no-shows—in fact, you can expect only 60 percent of your appointments to be met. With a well-filled schedule, then, I don't have huge gaps of time even if several clients don't show up. (Don't worry about chasing down the no-shows. You don't want tenants who don't keep appointments.) Second, by keeping appointments close together, renters see others coming and going. There's nothing like a little foot traffic to lend a sense of urgency to the process and create a great buzz about the property!

Word of mouth can be a good way to reach prospective tenants, so do let friends, family and colleagues know that you have an apartment for rent. But be careful about renting to family and friends. Your income suite is a business for you, and it can be tricky when your personal life and your business intersect.

THE TENANT APPLICATION AND THE TOUR

Believe me, a detailed application form can be a windfall of helpful info, but nothing beats a little listening and old-fashioned eavesdropping when sizing up tenants. For that reason, I always make sure that I have another person present during the appointments. That way, one of us can have people fill out an application, while the other shows the unit to the renters who have finished their forms.

When conducting tours, I allow folks to take pictures and to spend as much time as they need to look around. Prospective tenants often want a few moments alone as well to discuss the property amongst themselves. But as we go, I keep my ears open and make notes. You can often get a feel for what people will be like as tenants by the things they let slip and the questions they ask on the tour. Years ago, I showed a five-bedroom house to four young men. They seemed like pleasant, responsible guys, and I had no issues with renting a five-bedroom unit to only four people. Until, that is, they began discussing that fifth bedroom. "This is great," one of them said. "There's enough space here for a full drum kit—and a keyboard!" While they might have loved their new music studio, I was pretty sure that others in the building wouldn't. Paying a little attention saved me, and my other tenants, a bundle on Excedrin.

An application that gets the scoop will include:
- employment details;
- salary and banking info;
- references, including names of previous landlords;
- a list of everyone who will be living there;
- whether the applicant smokes;
- whether the applicant has pets.

Application templates are available from the Canada Mortgage and Housing Corporation website (www.cmhc.ca) and from provincial landlords groups like Ontario's Landlord's Self-Help Centre (www.landlordselfhelp.com). Also check out the CMHC website and your provincial human rights legislation (links can be found at www.unac.org/rights/actguide/canada) for guidelines about what questions landlords can and can't pose to potential tenants.

A LITTLE CHECKING, A LITTLE JUDGMENT GOES A LONG WAY

Did you meet a dream tenant on appointment day? Or someone who was clearly head and shoulders above the others? When that happens, it's hard not to make an on-the-spot decision. But take my word for it: bad idea! Make sure you see everyone who has made an appointment, and then review your notes and the applications. You really can't cut corners here if you want tenants who will pay their rent on time, keep your income suite clean and tidy, and respect you and your neighbours. Verify the information on the applications, including running credit checks and talking with references.

But while doing due diligence is essential, don't underestimate the importance of trusting your gut. Being a good judge of character is a fantastic asset for a landlord. I once showed one of my properties to a young woman who was enthusiastic about the newly renovated, upmarket space. I thought she might be a good fit for the place—until I read through her application. The email address she provided started with "partygirl69." *Really?* It was nice to know that she had an active social life, but I moved *that* application over to the reject pile.

So screening your tenants often comes down to keeping your eyes and ears open. Did some prospective tenants show up in a car filled with fast-food bags and cigarette butts? That might be what your income suite looks like in a few months. Did others have all of the necessary information at hand? Good organizational skills probably mean that rent will get paid on time and the apartment will get the care it needs. Did one couple seem especially suited to the place or the neighbourhood? If so, they may have a strong incentive to be reliable, long-term tenants. When all of the basic checks have come out positive, trust your instincts to choose the right tenant for your income suite.

THE AGREEMENT

So you've found a great tenant! Now it's time to confirm that he or she wants the unit and arrange to have the lease signed. (Don't call the unsuccessful applicants until you've finished the paperwork with your first choice. If that tenant falls through for some reason, you want to be able to go to the next person on your list.) A year-long lease is customary. That minimizes your paperwork and reduces the potential number of tenants in and out of an apartment.

Once the lease has been signed, call the other applicants in the order in which they came in. If anyone is upset, you can tell them that, all things being equal, you gave the rental to the first party who completed an application.

ESTABLISHING A GREAT LANDLORD-TENANT RELATIONSHIP

Attracting and choosing tenants is really just the first step in a great rental arrangement. As a landlord, you need to be proactive and in control *after* the lease is signed as well as before. And you can keep yourself in the driver's seat with a few simple acts.

When the tenants move in, I like to leave a small gift for them in their new apartment—a handwritten card and a bottle of wine, for instance. On the card, I'll include my contact info and encourage the tenants to be in touch if they encounter any problems or they need anything.

If I do hear from my tenants, I make sure that I respond quickly and effectively. I can't stress too much the importance of this kind of reciprocity. How you treat your tenants will dictate how they treat the property. It really is up to you.

A warm welcome and a quick response when they call are just a couple of ways to set the tone of the landlord-tenant relationship. Another good way to put yourself in control here is to give your tenants a little extra incentive to care for the property. Some landlords try to get a security deposit from tenants to cover any damage that might occur during the rental period. But that's a bad idea for two reasons. First, it is illegal in Canada. And second (if that wasn't enough to convince you), a security deposit requirement doesn't work very well. Demanding money up front strikes a mistrustful, punitive tone between landlord and tenant. Rather than starting off on that sour note, I make my rents slightly higher than the market value. But I use that extra income to provide for an offer in the rental agreement to "buy back" the keys when they move out, if the property is in good shape. It works like a charm. I am always aware that I take the lead in the rental relationship—if I am a responsible, attentive landlord, there's an excellent chance I will have responsible, attentive tenants. And this golden rule seems to be working: I've had over 10,000 tenants but have never had to evict anyone!

Even if you have done a great job of choosing your tenants, things can go wrong. Sometimes tenants' financial situations change and the monthly cheques no longer clear the bank. In situations like these, I move quickly. I will offer tenants a less expensive property if I have one available, or I will try to strike a deal: if they agree to find somewhere else to live within 60 days, I will wipe out the debt they have to me and will give them a reference saying that we parted on neutral terms. Most tenants are pleased to be able to get out of a lease they can no longer afford with their credit and their reputation intact.

Many provinces have independent agencies (like Ontario's Rent Check Credit Bureau: www.rentcheckcorp.com) that provide links to credit bureaus as well as information about tenants who have failed to pay rent, have criminal records or have damaged property. Some provinces have landlord advocacy associations that may be able to provide information about potential renters.

Chapter 9

GETTING YOUR HOME READY FOR SALE

In a sense, this entire book has been about getting your home ready to put on the market. Most of the major things you can do to improve your home are not last-minute fixes, and if increasing your home's value has been part of your long-term planning, you will have made the kinds of upgrades to your kitchen, bathroom, windows and doors that attract homebuyers and command the highest resale price.

But there is also some fine-tuning you can do immediately before you plan to sell that will make sure your home shows to its greatest advantage and gets you the top dollar.

In the introduction, I talked about keeping a record of all the home improvements you've done and photographing the work in progress as well as the finished work. Now is the time to assemble all of this documentation to prove to prospective buyers that your home is in tip-top shape. Organize photos, renovation contracts, inspection reports, energy audits, warranties and bills of sale for things like your garage doors, roofs, windows, furnaces or appliances in a binder that can be shown to buyers and real estate agents. If you have a site plan, have that available as well. If the new owners are thinking of doing any major renovations, they will need one, and knowing that this is part of the deal can set their minds at ease. Remember to include photos of your gardens and exterior property in all seasons.

Cracked concrete steps or paving will be a red flag to buyers that serious work may be needed on the property. Make sure that you take care of this kind of repair before you list your home.

Next you'll want to prep or stage your house so that it shows well. This means decluttering and depersonalizing the entire house and arranging furniture to suggest comfort and space. You can either do this yourself, or you can hire a professional house stager.

When you are hiring a professional, you can opt for one of two levels of staging. The least expensive option involves using your own furniture and adding or replacing some of your pieces with "fake" furniture. A stager can rent props like blow-up mattresses, plastic TVs, cardboard dining room chairs with cloth covers, paintings and rugs. This may sound odd, but the props look very real in pictures, and since homebuyers are walking through rooms, not lying in the beds or eating at the table, the overall effect of the props works well.

A more expensive version of staging involves renting real furniture and quality decorative pieces. All types of staging (even when you do it yourself) may require you to rent storage space to house furniture and personal items that you need to take out of your home to show it to its best advantage. Professional staging usually costs a minimum of several thousand dollars a month. How do you decide whether it is worth it? If the cost for staging is less than about three-quarters of one percent of the value of the house, it may be worth the expenditure (for example, $3,000 or less for a $400,000 home). And what if your home is in an area where houses tend to be on the market for more than a month? You might be surprised to hear that it may still be worth it to stage your home for one month only. While it is staged, you can get photographs to use in your listing and in any brochures you produce. That attractive listing will draw more people to your home, and more traffic means the higher likelihood of a good offer. You can also put the pictures on display or in a binder in your home, so even if the rented furniture has gone back, buyers can get a sense of what the home *could* look like. And if you have a rental suite in your home, you definitely want to have pictures of the unit looking its best. I stage all of my rental properties (usually for only a week) and use the pictures from the original staging each time I list the unit. With the photos in hand, prospective tenants can get a good idea of the potential of the space, even if they are walking through an empty apartment.

Staging your house can draw potential buyers' attention to its strong points—a sure way to make them want to call it "home."

Here are a few other tips and tricks to make your home show at its best:

- Make sure all walls and ceilings have a fresh coat of neutral paint.

- Remove family photos and any idiosyncratic or unusual artworks or decor. Clear your fridge door of magnets, art, notices or any other bits and pieces.

- Repair any cracks or stains on the walls and ceilings and remove any evidence of previous problems. Don't, however, mask problems or hand issues down to the new owners. Make sure any outstanding issues have been fixed. The home should be in good repair when you show it and when you hand over the keys.

- Use bed linens and bath towels that are neutral in colour. New white towels always help to make a bathroom look fresh and clean.

- Clear out closets and cupboards. Highlight storage spaces. You don't need these to be empty, but they need to look as if they are more than adequate to hold an owner's belongings. In a linen closet, for example, the shelves might hold a few sets of neatly folded sheets and a number of towels, but not be stuffed to the ceiling. Likewise, your clothes closets can have clothes in them, but not have hangers wedged against hangers and clothes ready to spill out.

- Make sure kitchen and bathroom countertops are clear of clutter. Remove small appliances, baby bottles and anything else that personalizes the area and covers up work spaces. The same holds true for bureau tops and desktops.

- Wash all of your windows inside and out and keep mirrors sparkling clean.

- Clean the top of your water heater, washer and dryer, and other fixtures in your laundry room, electrical room and basement. If the places in a home that are ordinarily a little dirty or overlooked are tidy and clean instead, prospective buyers will be convinced that you have taken good care of the home.

- Unfinished basements should be as empty and clear as possible to show the potential of the space for storage or finishing. If you have filled your basement with boxes and other items, it will look smaller and darker to prospective buyers and may even

suggest that you are covering up damp floors or crumbling foundation walls. The same holds true for garages. If you have a double or triple garage, make sure that all of the parking spaces are clear and empty.

- If there is any dampness in the home at all, run a dehumidifier. A feeling of dryness throughout the house, and particularly in the basement, is a subtle way of emphasizing the good condition of the building.

- Clean all of your appliances inside and out. Gleaming fridges, stovetops, ovens and laundry machines tend to look new, even if they aren't.

- If your hardwood floors are a bit squeaky, sprinkle talcum powder in the cracks. Allow it to sit for about a day so that it settles into the crevices and grooves, and then vacuum up the remainder. The talc will act as a lubricant between the strips of wood and reduce the squeakiness of the floor when it is walked on.

- If any of your screen doors tend to slam shut, adjust the screw at the base of the pump so the door closes more slowly. Most people assume a slamming screen door is broken (and is therefore something they will have to replace) when usually it only needs a little adjusting.
- Keep the garden weeded, the lawn mown and the driveway and walkways shovelled while your house is on the market.

ASSESSING POTENTIAL FOR INCREASED VALUE WHEN BUYING REAL ESTATE

Shopping for a home can be a hugely stressful and emotional experience. There are so many things to consider: neighbourhood, schools, space, age and condition of the house, gardens and so on. Because of all this, many people are overly influenced by the aesthetics of a house. If things look clean, new and decorated in a fashion they like—if, in other words, they can see themselves moving right in and not doing a thing other than arranging furniture—they love the place. But this is a shortsighted approach that can severely limit the growth of your real estate investment. To get the best bang for your buck, and to increase the return on investment that you make in your home in a truly dramatic way, you have to be able to clearly and unemotionally assess a property's potential. Are the house's weaknesses largely cosmetic—something a few cans of paint could easily fix? Is the house priced low enough that you could afford some major renovations? Is there space for an income suite?

Many people don't think about a house's potential to increase in value with the right renovations or changes. If you keep these considerations in mind as you go house hunting, you will be able to spot the real bargain properties on the market and maximize the return on your real estate investment.

PARTING THOUGHTS

You should now have plenty of ideas and tools for increasing the value of your home or your investment property. And you should have a good sense of what work you might do on your own and what you will want to hire professionals to do. But there's one other thing to consider when you are making your home improvement plans.

I've talked about the importance of planning and quality materials and work throughout the book. And I've talked quite a lot about cost. What I haven't addressed, however, is time—one of the key components in any renovation. Time, price and quality: the truth is that, when renovating, you can only ever have two of those things. If you want a job done quickly and with high quality, it is going to cost you more. Or you may be able to save money, but you will have to sacrifice either time or quality. Often your best choice is some balance of the three factors. But homeowners have an advantage over flippers and contractors, who need to get work done quickly so that they aren't carrying a property for too long: with many home improvements, you can live in your home with no extra costs during the duration of the work, so time is not such a crucial factor.

Whatever way you decide to juggle those elements, if you follow the three keys to home improvements—quality, consistency of space and upgrades that are in line with the value of your property—your changes and renos should contribute significantly to the appreciation of your house and get you the highest dollar on resale, making you not only a proud home-owner but also a savvy investor.

INDEX